STUDENTS ABROAD:
STRANGERS AT HOME

STUDENTS ABROAD: STRANGERS AT HOME

Education for a Global Society

by

NORMAN L. KAUFFMANN

JUDITH N. MARTIN

HENRY D. WEAVER

with

JUDY WEAVER

For information, contact:
Intercultural Press, Inc.
P.O. Box 700
Yarmouth, Maine 04096, USA

Book design by Jacques Chazaud
Cover design by LetterSpace

Printed in the United States of America.

97 96 94 93 92 1 2 3 4 5 6

Library of Congress Cataloging-in-Publication Data

Students abroad, strangers at home : education for a global society / by Norman L. Kauffman . . . [et al.].
p. cm.
Includes bibliographical references (p.).
ISBN 0-933662-94-7 : $19.95
1. Foreign study—United States—Case studies.
2. International education—United States—Case studies.
I. Kauffmann, Norman L.
LB2376.S76 1991
370.19′6—dc20 91-38527
CIP

CONTENTS

INTRODUCTION 1

CHAPTER 1: STUDENTS ABROAD 5

Don 6
Lori 12
Karen 18
Matt 25

CHAPTER 2: INTELLECTUAL DEVELOPMENT ABROAD 33

Learning a Foreign Language 35
Gaining a New Perspective on the Major 41
Increasing Knowledge in General Studies 44
The Quality of Foreign Courses and the Problem of Credit 48

CHAPTER 3: DEVELOPING AN INTERNATIONAL PERSPECTIVE 55

Changes in Perception of Host Country 58
Preexisting Attitudes and Expectations 61
Length of Stay 62

Immersion in the Host Culture *63*
Location of Study Abroad *66*
Change in Perceptions of the Home Culture *68*
Global Understanding *74*
Knowledge Acquisition *76*
Affective Change *79*
Behavioral Change *85*

CHAPTER 4: PERSONAL DEVELOPMENT ABROAD *91*

Intrapersonal Development *99*
Interpersonal Development *105*
Development of Values *110*
Development of Life Direction/Vocation *112*
Personal Development and Reentry *115*

CHAPTER 5: EDUCATION AS CHANGE *123*

A Model of the Transformation Process *127*
Autonomy *127*
Belonging *130*
Values *134*
Cognition *136*
Vocation *138*
Worldview *140*
Summary of the Model *142*
Implications of the Model *143*

CHAPTER 6: STUDY ABROAD AND INTERNATIONALIZATION OF THE UNIVERSITY: RECOMMENDATIONS FOR ACTION *147*

Foreign Languages Must Be Taken Seriously *149*
General Studies Programs Need to Include Study Abroad *150*
Majors Can Be Enriched by Study Abroad *152*
Maintaining Quality in Study Abroad *155*
Reintegrating Students into Home Institution *157*

APPENDIX *161*
BIBLIOGRAPHY *187*

INTRODUCTION

Colleges and universities today are faced with a major problem of the type that comes only when one epoch ends and another begins. That problem is *how to make a university education relevant in a global society.*

During the last forty years we have moved from a world in which society, commerce, and education were defined within the context of nation-states to one in which they are increasingly perceived as part of a global community.

Products from all parts of the world are used daily by people from the most developed to the least developed nations. It is a world of fax machines, international TV news coverage, instantaneous electronic communication, and rapid air travel. Academic research is interconnected with the work of other scholars throughout the world. In short, the global village is here.

In response, faculty and administrators in higher education are searching for ways that will bring our educational programs into the global era. How, they are asking, do we internationalize our colleges and universities? *It is the thesis of this book that study abroad is one of the most powerful tools available for internationalizing the curriculum in American colleges and universities.*

In preparing this volume, the authors began by examining the research regarding the effects of studying abroad on participating students (Weaver 1989). They then interviewed students from the three institutions with which they are affiliated in order to find real case histories that would attach the research results to reality and make them more understandable. In the process they identified two key variables which determine the degree to which a sojourn abroad affects students: the student's maturity and the extent to which the student is immersed in the host culture.

Consequently, in chapter 1 the study begins with the presentation of the stories of four students who personally had reached different levels of maturity at the time they went abroad and who experienced different degrees of immersion in the culture in which they studied.

The next three chapters focus on the three major areas in which study abroad is considered to have an impact: (1) intellectual development (including language learning), (2) expanded international perspectives, and (3) personal development.

In chapter 2 three ways in which students develop intellectually when abroad are discussed: (1) through language study, (2) through courses in their majors which offer them new perspectives on the subject, and (3) through the acquisition of knowledge in broad, general areas of study which increase the individual's capacity to think systematically and critically (which is akin to the goals of what is often referred to as "general studies"). How course work done overseas is assessed and given credit within the structure of the American academic system is also discussed.

The third chapter examines the manner in which students develop an international perspective when studying abroad.

The literature on the subject is carefully surveyed, and three basic ways in which students change are identified: (1) in the perception they have of the host culture and in their understanding of it, (2) in the way they perceive their own culture, and (3) in what the authors call "global understanding."

The fourth chapter explores how the personal development of students studying abroad is measured and how it relates to developmental psychology. In studies done on the subject, discrepancies have been found among the results of measurements using standardized tests, specially constructed instruments, and self-reporting surveys. These discrepancies are discussed and explained.

In chapter 5 the authors propose a theoretical framework based on the work of Piaget and Inhelder (1958), for understanding the effects of study abroad on students. In this view—of education as change—the growth resulting from an overseas study experience is a complex evolving process of balancing and rebalancing, of assimilating (interpreting new experiences in terms of current or previous structures of knowing) and accommodating (modifying existing ways of looking at the world to incorporate new knowledge or experience).

The conclusion to be reached is not only that study abroad is potentially a powerful educational technique, but that the design of the program and the selection of the participants can also make a significant difference in a program's outcome. Therefore, the final chapter offers a number of recommendations which the authors feel will expand the opportunities for an increase in effectiveness of study abroad programs in American educational institutions. The salient research to which the authors have referred throughout the book is summarized in a table in the appendix.

CHAPTER ONE

STUDENTS ABROAD

This chapter presents case studies of four typical study abroad students, demonstrating how differences in the students themselves and in the programs in which they participate can result in different outcomes. The details of these students' cases, along with excerpts from interviews with other students, will be used in subsequent chapters to illustrate research findings. As for the students, Don, who knew little about the country to which he was going but was open to new experiences, grew dramatically both personally and academically. Lori, who also was unfamiliar with her host country but was less adaptable, gained little from the experience. The third student, Karen, more mature but with no previous experience abroad, developed somewhat personally and gained a significant intellectual understanding of the country in which she studied. Finally, Matt, both more mature and with previous experience abroad, reached the highest level of intellectual and academic sophistication. In this chapter as well as in those that follow, all the students that were interviewed are quoted with their permission and last names have been withheld to protect their identities.

DON

Before his trip to Costa Rica, Don knew exactly what he wanted out of life. He wanted to be rich. He had been reared in an upper-middle-class family in Maryland and steeped in the Protestant work ethic from early childhood. "I thought I had to have a tremendous drive for monetary reward," he said.

In spite of this belief, Don did not feel drawn toward any particular vocation as he began his studies at Goshen College, a liberal arts school in northern Indiana operated by the Mennonite Church. "I was not a very self-confident or outgoing person. There were certain times when I was worked up, I would make my presence known, but generally I was quiet and shy." He believed that people based their acceptance of him on his material or academic success, and he wasn't sure he had enough of either.

But something happened to Don which changed all that. His ideas of success, personal worth, friendship, and family all underwent a major shift.

The college Don had chosen required, as part of its general studies curriculum, a term of study and service in a foreign country, called the "Study Service Term" (SST). Don did not want to go. Although he knew every student was supposed to participate, he also knew that exceptions were sometimes made. He looked for a way out.

> I was very hesitant about SST when I first came to Goshen College. I was, in fact, very determined that I was not going to go. Well, the time finally came, and I was scheduled to go last spring. About a month before departure, I started to really get scared. I had been going through a lot of changes in my life. With these changes and this great fear of the unexpected, I made a commitment to Christ. At that point I was able to let go of a large part of that fear and to set the stage for a good experience.

In the spring Don joined his group of some twenty-five students and together they traveled by bus and airplane to San José, Costa Rica. The Goshen group was a homogeneous one; most of the students were in their late teens or early twenties and were from Mennonite or other Protestant homes in the Midwest. Few had ever traveled outside the United States. Historic San José, with its Catholic, Spanish-speaking inhabitants and its mountain setting, was amazing to them.

"There was a whole different atmosphere," said Don. "The size of the houses. Everything! To put it bluntly, it was an adjustment." At first, Don felt most shocked by the lack of material wealth in Costa Rica, where the per capita income is a quarter that of the United States.

> I really got a new perspective on the world and on my own life. When you are living in the United States, you can have about anything you want. You can go out to the stores and get whatever you wish. You have many freedoms. When you go to another country, especially a Third-World one, you see how they live, how very unindustrialized the nation is from an economic standpoint, and the difference in the way people live.
>
> It was interesting to see that our middle class is equal to their upper class.... I always had things better than most of the students in our group. For me it was especially difficult to make that adjustment. I lived with Costa Rican families from the middle class. What they considered very special, I considered routine. I had to learn. They gave me the beef and other special food items that they themselves couldn't afford to eat. They gave me a single room while the one son and father shared a room. I had to realize that their giving this to me was a value they prized greater than having a room alone for themselves.

During the first half of their three-month term in Costa Rica, the students in Don's group lived in San José and studied Spanish and the local culture. Don said he drew strength from his fellow students for the initial adjustments.

> The group provided the bridge into the culture. It was a vital support until we got enough self-confidence, knowledge, and experience to be on our own with our families and to be immersed more fully.

> An analogy would be wading into the water before you dive in.

For the second half of the term, the students were sent individually to smaller towns to live and work among the people.

Don discovered, to his amazement, that he could adjust, and with that knowledge came a new confidence.

> I made it! I got used to eating rice and beans every day. You get used to things after awhile. The neatest thing ... is to know that I could adjust to all this and I didn't have to have the plushness and the luxury that I had become accustomed to in the United States.
>
> More importantly, what happens if the economy of the United States collapses and we all are in poverty? I am not going to break, I'm still going to be me. I'll be able to adapt to that. That really is a good feeling and it gives you a different perspective on life, the way you treat other people and the way you view the future.

On his own in Golfito, a town of about twelve thousand, Don began to change in deep, personal ways.

> I became a much more outgoing, social, and a more confident person.... That was the most important change. SST provided the environment for this change. I finally began to get ahold of this in a way that really began to change me.
>
> I had an excellent family and they helped me a great deal, even with my Spanish. They were very upstanding members of their community. They were devout Catholics and that helped. I was forced to interact with other people and to make friends.

> I learned that the people accepted me for who I was and for myself. [In the U.S.] I never had quite that view of acceptance. . . . The people [of Costa Rica] are really down to earth and they are not pretentious, at least not in the middle and lower classes.
>
> The sense of family is tremendous there. I was really drawn in, treated as a member. The bonds that bound us together were terrific. I was extremely close to my second family, and they contributed most to the changes in me. They very much helped me to become myself, to express my feelings.

As his Costa Rican experience came to an end and Don headed for home, he was unaware of the rocky reentry that awaited him. "I didn't know that it was normal at that time," he explained. Seeing his U.S. home through Central American eyes stunned him.

> It seemed to me that we had so much waste and so many things that we really didn't need. My family in the U.S. is very active. The people in Costa Rica are really laid back. They don't have schedules or things like that. I got home and it was like a madhouse. Well, it's always a madhouse, but I wasn't used to it. We had people coming and going. . . . There was always something happening. I had lived with this before, but coming back from Costa Rica, I just couldn't handle it. It literally wiped me out, and I slept for a day and a half. My family couldn't believe it. . . . I was shot. Moving from the Costa Rican pace of life to this was just emotionally and physically exhausting.
>
> After that I was really grouchy. It was good to be back, but I didn't feel the strong ties that I once

> did. Maybe that was upsetting, that I didn't feel the close ties that I did with my family in Costa Rica. Here was my natural family and I didn't feel as close.

Gradually, Don found his way back into family life, but in a new way.

> I had to get back into the family on different terms. I don't think they expected all the changes or the magnitude of growth that really happened. The only time that we really sat down and talked about what happened to me was the first two or three hours that I was back.

A year later, Don had begun to find ways to reconcile the lessons he learned in Costa Rica with the enduring values of his upbringing. While he no longer saw financial success as his highest goal, he said "I still am a very ambitious person and want to be successful at what I do." He had also lost his fear of failure and was therefore willing to take risks. "If I would go into personal bankruptcy, I know that I could live the way I did in Costa Rica. It would be distressing, but I know I would adjust to it." As an example, Don cited his reaction to an advertisement for an inexpensive trip to Mexico. "I wasn't afraid to go for it because I now know I could make it. Two years ago I never would have given it consideration."

Don was still undecided about a career. However, since returning from Costa Rica, he found he was more motivated to study and had raised his grade point average. He was looking for a "middle way" between the American work ethic of his parents and the Costa Rican attention to interpersonal relationships. He was searching for a balance between the "materialistic values [of the United States] that drive everybody to the extreme, where you are measured by your financial and academic success, and a laid-back society [Costa Rica] where you don't get anything accomplished."

He will not forget Costa Rica because, as he said simply, "This SST experience profoundly changed my life."

LORI

If she could hear Don describe the riches he found in Costa Rica, Lori might feel jealous. Lori was also a Goshen College student who studied abroad during a spring term, but her experience was vastly different from Don's. She was the student who didn't "make it." For her, the adventure of study abroad turned into a frightening and difficult time, and she was relieved when it was over.

Why are some U.S. students successful abroad while others struggle and long for home? Lori searched for answers after her return. Her musings were imbued with a sense of guilt over what should have been. Often she tried to justify her behavior, but she was also capable of insight into both her own shortcomings and the circumstances involved in her term abroad, which she sadly labeled "a bummer."

Lori's experience will help illustrate some of the hindrances to learning and maturing on foreign shores. She failed to expand her horizons in any direction. Immature and suspicious, she resisted personal growth. Nor did she gain an understanding of her foreign hosts and their culture.

Lori was sent to the French-speaking island of Guadeloupe in the West Indies, where she started out with high expectations. She had understood from fellow students at Goshen that SST was supposed to be "the most wonderful thing in the world." Unlike Don, however, she had not gone through any predeparture soul-searching and preparation.

On the contrary, Lori thought the benefits of study abroad would fall into her lap, without any risk or work on her part.

> I was disappointed that it was so much harder than I thought it would be. My first six weeks were really pretty hard. I was angry, depressed and discouraged. What made it worse was that I didn't want to be. When you think you shouldn't be feeling negative and you are, that makes things even worse.

Mindful of the high marks the SST program had received from other Goshen students, Lori felt frustrated—even cheated—that it was not working for her. She came to see each new challenge not as a chance for growth but rather as further proof that everything was working against her.

Yet, she was later able to identify some of the reasons for starting out on the wrong foot. "Part of the difficulty was not knowing the language very well, and that was because I had only taken a semester of French before I went. Also I am not that great of a communicator even in my own culture." Lori's host family for the first half of the term spoke English, but this hindered rather than helped her.

> They wanted to talk to us in English and we wanted to talk to them in French. I felt put down when I tried to talk French with them. However, the members of my second family were more country people and you could just say anything and if it wasn't correct grammatically, it didn't really matter because no one cared.... I felt more comfortable trying in that situation and I learned the most there.

Lori noticed that some students found ways to reach out and to learn without knowing a lot of French.

> I would say that the people who got the most out of the experience were those who could communicate the best and those who didn't know French very well but could communicate anyway.

She believed that she was not a very mature or adaptable person when she arrived in Guadeloupe. "It takes me longer to get used to surroundings and adjust than the average person," she said. While Don was impressed and humbled by the generosity of his SST host family, Lori felt cramped.

> I missed being able to do things for myself. It was hard to tell your family that you wanted to . . . cook tonight, or go out and do something on your own, to be responsible for yourself. They thought they had to be good hosts, which is fine, but sometimes that gets old—to always, always be given to and treated like a guest. A lot of the time it felt like being a child again. You are at a stage where you have just become more independent and you have to move back and be more dependent.

She had the same reaction when the faculty leader tried to encourage the students to immerse themselves in Guadeloupan culture.

> At first we as a group felt nagged at to get into the culture. It sort of made us resist it and feel rebellious. We didn't want to be told what we were supposed to be doing or feeling.

Lori's group had another problem.

> We were an older group. I lived with another SSTer and she just wanted to go home. She was trying her

> best, but she had a lot of strong ties at home and was trying to overcome her homesickness, but that worked against me and pulled me down also.... There were probably ten students that were able to get into the culture, whether they knew the language or not. They didn't have the feeling that they wanted to be somewhere else. They were just themselves. Fourteen of us struggled in some form and never really quite got into it.... I think it is a lot harder when you are older. One girl was engaged, and there were several people who were done with college except for SST.... For them SST was just something to get out of the way, to get done.

In spite of these things which held her back, Lori did begin to relax as time went on. Although her group was not supportive, she found a friend, Becky, who was.

> I kept a journal, but we did not talk much as a group. I did talk to Becky. I think a lot of the group felt the way I did. So I did have some outlet for that. I felt understood by Becky.

For the second half of the trimester, Lori was sent with one other student to a small town, where they worked in a children's day-care center. This period, she said, was a little better:

> The family left us more on our own and they made more of an effort to understand us. I was also with a different SSTer who was pretty fluent in French and that helped me get into the culture a lot more.

Lori had a strong sense that her duty as a student abroad was to dive into the language and culture of Guadeloupe. "To get into the culture" is how she put it, a yardstick held up to each episode of her stay. Yet, unlike her fellow student, Don, she did not speak of what she learned, of a "new perspective," or of changes in her values, her interactions with others, her view of the world and of the future. What Lori described is how she built a shell to keep herself intact.

It began, perhaps, because of the attention North American women often receive from men in Latin America.

> We got so tired of the males bothering us. Initially, after I was back and would see a person of the opposite sex, it would just bring back the ways of coping down there. You had a tendency to look away ... or develop this look that you gave them.... You just developed a shell to keep things like that out.

Lori's shell kept out other uncomfortable things as well.

> There are poor people, but you just don't see that. Some of the poor have the most elaborate cabinets in their little tin shack, or humongous TVs, or a nice car outside. I didn't meet any people who didn't have homes. I did see someone washing clothes by a fountain out by the street. The people don't like you to see that kind of thing. They discourage you from trying to see that. Poverty is there, but I don't think it changed my views of homeless people or poverty in America.

Her views on religion also went without scrutiny.

> I don't think my experience there changed my religious beliefs at all. I never went to a Catholic service

while I was there, and that was the main religion of the country. Both my [host] families were Catholic.

In my second family the mother was a real character. She was the superstitious Catholic, the stereotypical Catholic, the one who would cross herself when she would walk in front of [the statue of] St. Anne—you know, bad luck and everything. She wasn't like an American Catholic. You don't expect American Catholics to be like that.

We never attended services because we really didn't feel invited. They never invited us to come along, although probably if we had asked, they would have taken us, but we really didn't feel welcome to do so.

Lori identified one experience in Guadeloupe that did mature her: her work in the day-care center. She said she was able to build confidence in her chosen field of education.

I think working in that daycare did make me think, "Well, I can do that." So I guess the job I have now [in a U.S. daycare] is sort of because I worked in a daycare there. . . . I guess I felt pretty unsure of myself when I was working at the daycare down there. I wasn't really sure what my role was. I couldn't just ask a question when it popped into my mind because of the lack of language. You just had to do what you saw other people doing and hope that it was right. But now, working here I feel pretty confident of handling whatever comes up because I have come through student teaching as well as SST.

Lori's improved self-assurance also helped her overcome some shyness.

> When you have made it through SST, you think you can handle a lot of things that you couldn't before. For instance, when I came back, I would be in a store and want to know something. Before SST I would never have had the nerve to ask. Now, it's no big deal, you can talk in English, so why not go ask?

Beyond this, however, her time in Guadeloupe appeared not to have changed her deeply. She said she had no real problems of adjustment upon return. Interestingly, like Don, she slept long hours when she got home, not because the pace of North American life was overwhelming but because she needed to release tension.

> I had been under such mental and physical stress for so long that when I got home, I said, "OK, you can let go now," and I just slept.

After resting Lori said she "felt fine."

Perhaps the best way to sum up Lori's experience abroad is in a question she asked, one that lingers in the minds of many students after they return home: "I felt a little bit of regret leaving Guadeloupe. Feelings like, had I done all the things that I could have done? Had I wasted an opportunity?"

KAREN

Like Lori, Karen, a student at the University of California, Santa Barbara, began her trip abroad with several strikes against her. Her study abroad destination was France, which some researchers consider one of the most challenging countries for U.S. students. Furthermore, she described herself as painfully shy, and she got little support from her fellow American students; it was a difficult, factional group. Yet her summary of her time abroad was "Really good, really bad, really hard. It was really a good experience."

Hard but good: perhaps the ideal description of a study abroad experience. How did Karen reach that conclusion?

To begin with, she possessed an openness for the cross-cultural experience that Lori lacked. Karen was already in love with learning new languages. She was majoring in French and Spanish and had won an award for being the best foreign languages student. However, she had never been abroad; in fact, she had never even been away from home. As her junior year approached, she was still living at home with her mother. Karen knew that as a language major, it was important for her to spend some time abroad. The time for a make-or-break experience had arrived.

French was edging out Spanish as her primary interest, so Karen decided to spend her junior year in France. Her mother encouraged her to go. Karen explained, "She wanted me to get out and be with people my own age." Karen asked to go to the city of Poitiers because she had been told that the spoken French there was more conservative, or "pure." She said "I went there for that reason, and because it was small. It was the first time I had gone away from home."

When she arrived, Karen found that her fellow students from California were not as satisfied to be in Poitiers as she was. They had been assigned to the small country town because the more popular and cosmopolitan cities already had too many students. "The other students didn't necessarily want to be in Paris, but maybe Montpellier, because it was near the beach," she said.

Karen and another student moved in with a French family. After completing the required intensive language study, the Americans began regular university classes along with the French students. "I think the first two or three months were the hardest, and Thanksgiving was hard," Karen remembered. "We were all sort of homesick at that time." The French students, accustomed to seeing groups of Americans come and go, were not friendly. "We were in freshman classes," Karen said. "We were juniors and they were freshmen.... And they were very immature in class. They talked all the time, just incredibly rude."

Some of her classes were very demanding. She hated her literature class.

> It was really hard to go. It was Tuesday at eight o'clock in the morning, and the students were not friendly at all.... She was intimidating, that teacher. I think maybe it was just her mannerisms. She was very old school. She reminded me of a Catholic nun!

A class in international law, although difficult, turned out to be a good experience.

> It was the best class I had all year.... That's the class I learned the most vocabulary in.... It made me a better student because I had to work harder to be at the same level that I was at home. I don't think I had a problem grasping the material so much as actually sitting down and reading. Some of those books for the law class were really hard. That was sometimes discouraging. The professor talked a mile a minute and he never stopped. The first two months we did not understand a word he said. I'm not joking! And he smoked; they all smoked in class. Six Americans just sitting there. We would put our pens down, just look at him, and then go back and piece together words. It was very phonetic. The French students helped us. Some of them

> were friendly, some of them weren't. But, I think on the whole they were more friendly than in other classes.

As time passed, the positive outweighed the negative. By Christmas, Karen was no longer homesick and even found the courage to travel alone to visit friends in Germany and Spain.

She had survived the initial culture shock and felt comfortable with French life. She gave credit to the atmosphere in Poitiers and to her host family.

> There's a definite difference between Paris and the province. Poitiers is very different. The people there were warmer. They were much more welcoming. And I'm glad that it was a smaller city. I think maybe that's why I was able to integrate so fast. There's not much to do, the roads are twisty and winding, but you learn them very quickly.
>
> I think living with a family was the best thing for me and the other guy from UCSB who lived there. We had a pact to speak only French because it would have been really easy for us to speak English all the time. So if we spoke English, we had to put money in a pot. The family was really nice, very warm, very helpful. . . . They were quite wealthy. He [the father] was a very successful vet. They had a microwave oven, a VCR, and everything we didn't have at the time. I didn't think they would be so American. They'd had Americans [students] in their house for the last ten years.
>
> They were very patient and they had so many books; they were very helpful. They'd had five kids of their own. So they were even very familiar with

> our professors. The son had had the literature professor that we had.

The youngest son, who was close to the Americans in age, introduced them to his friends. He provided them with social contacts they would not have had otherwise.

> I had French friends, but not from school so much. We had a tutor for each class, a French tutor. The tutor from the international relations class was really good.
>
> His name was Hervé. He brought a lot of his friends and we did things together.... So it was through the family and through the international relations class that I met French people. And also through the [program's] liaison officer. She lived just half a block from our house. So we ended up doing a lot of things with her that we wouldn't normally have done—like going to the theater. It was her idea that we get a [theater] subscription. And she didn't speak any English.

Karen said her self-esteem was strengthened when she learned she had the ability to adapt. She accepted herself.

> I realized I was capable of doing more than I thought I was, because I was always really shy and afraid to do things. I still think I'm a timid person, but I am just quiet. I can do things, but in a quiet way, because I'm really stubborn!
>
> I got more self-confidence, I think, just by being away from my mother, having friends my own age, and just doing more things. The traveling helped, too.

Karen developed insights about international differences. "I learned not to take so much for granted and not to stereotype, to categorize people. It amazed me how modern—modern Western—my French family was." Karen said she matured "just by experiencing different things and meeting all types of people, not judging people too quickly, being able to deal with people even if you're unhappy to be there with them."

Karen applied her new perceptions on international relations to the interpersonal level, which enabled her to better communicate with the other American students.

> There were definite schisms in the group—about three groups, so we had more problems with ourselves than with the country.
>
> I really didn't like Americans while I was there. A lot of us pretended not to be Americans. Some of the tourists were so incredibly rude to people. It was embarrassing. You would get a lot more if you were polite and just kind of a normal person. There were a lot of brash Americans in places we went. There was one in our group, too. We changed her.
>
> We were very honest among ourselves, I think. We kept telling each other certain things. We weren't happy about it, but it was good to see how other people perceive you. Not necessarily to try to change because of them, but just to try to keep an even keel—not too American, not too French. There were a lot of kids in our group that tried to be French. I think that's a mistake because you can't.
>
> I knew I wasn't French. I could pretend sometimes, but it was a mistake going over thinking you were going to be French and fit in. It takes a long time and the students weren't overly friendly with us.

After a year, Karen felt she was only beginning. She knew that back home her mother was missing her, but she longed to stay.

> I was happy to be away. It was hard to come home. I didn't really want to come home at the time. I was thinking of staying another year, but then I didn't want to have to come back and finish my B.A. I thought I could get even more out of a second year because I was just beginning to really feel comfortable, and then I had to go home.

She did go home, though. Her short European hairstyle and black leather jacket suggested inner changes. Almost immediately, she returned to her annual summer job.

> I missed being in France. It was good being around people, getting back into the swing of things, but when I came home, I was a little disappointed. It seemed like I had done so much and changed so much and everything at work was exactly the same. No one had changed. It was like a time warp. It was a very strange feeling. It seemed to me, when I came home, that people were shocked; my hair was so short. But *I* was different.

Karen's mother provided a sympathetic ear, but some of her friends were less understanding. She learned from that experience. Shifting relationships meant "more culture shock when I came back than when I went. Some of it was good. I had a girlfriend, a so-called friend; we really drifted apart. It was tough. You learn a lot about people, I guess."

Karen finished her bachelor's degree in French and then went on to earn a master's in French literature. The classes and contact with students who had also been in Poitiers helped Karen maintain her language skills. "Those of us who had gone to France got together every other day, practically, in the pub and talked French. We didn't want to lose it." She still tries to keep in touch with her French family even though it is not easy. "They're not very good writers. I send them Christmas cards and tell them what I'm up to."

Karen believes her year in France helped her to mature and focus her academic career. But it did more than that. "On all levels you grow—it's so hard to explain. There's a lot more things I want to do, places I want to see. And I want to go back there."

MATT

Which type of student will get the most out of study abroad? While some, like the inexperienced Don and the shy Karen, were unexpected successes, others are predictable. Matt was one such student. He had all the ingredients for success.

Matt had already lived and worked in Germany, spoke several languages, and had traveled in other Arab countries before going to Tunisia during his junior year at the University of Minnesota. As a geography major, he yearned for international experiences and was mature enough to aspire to a level of immersion and understanding achieved by few.

But, while Matt had a good year and gained valuable insights into both his home and host cultures, it did not come easily. He found ways to transform difficulties into challenges, and hardships into achievements. Back in Minnesota, Matt continued to be challenged by an academic system he was convinced did not appreciate the value of his learning abroad.

Matt had studied Arabic for two and a half years in Minnesota. When he arrived in Tunis, he was ready to find ways to immerse himself in the Islamic culture, a society he considered as mysterious as it was closed to outsiders.

It was slow going and hard. He had trouble getting to know Tunisians, and many subjects were closed to him as a non-Muslim and a foreigner.

> It was difficult. Part of it was my own fault. Part of it was that Tunisians have very structured relationships with friends and relatives. They were happy to talk to me and I'd get invited to people's houses, but I never felt I was really accepted.
>
> In certain parts of Tunis there are mosques where women would go to pray and drink from a fountain to guarantee fertility. Or in the market, I'd see spices—like dried up chameleons on spikes—used in folk magic. I'd try to talk with my friends and ask them, "What's that for?" They'd just shrug it off. If I had been a woman and had asked an old woman, I'm sure she would have told me.

Matt knew that as a Westerner he could not expect much contact with Tunisian women.

> I remember going to visit a Tunisian family one afternoon with two American [women] friends of mine who were in the Peace Corps. They knew the wife and went immediately into the kitchen with the wife and I watched Italian TV with the men. That's usually how it was, and not being used to that—that was a problem.
>
> Tunisians were extremely friendly, but it would be hard to be integrated, immersed in the culture. If I had been actively trying to convert to Islam, or had more time, maybe. . . .

Even so, Matt estimated that by the end of his stay he was more immersed in Tunisian culture than most American students because of his travels within the country and his fluency in Arabic.

> You could talk to a Tunisian and speak French, but if you talked Arabic there was a connection. They knew you a little bit more, and you could talk with more Tunisians. When I was traveling in the south, I met some guys that worked for a tourist company, and all the foreigners they had met spoke French. I spoke Arabic with them and they were delighted and they sort of accepted me into their little group. They'd say something in French and English to other tourists and then in Arabic to me. I eventually got a ride back to Tunis with them. That was a real door-opener. I could have communicated in French, but it would have been different.

A third reason for his rich experience was that Matt moved from the dormitory at the Bourghiba Language Institute, where he was studying, to an Arab-style apartment in the traditional part of town called the *medina*.

> A high point was living in an area of the city that not many foreigners lived in. That was really valuable to me, living in the medina. Most foreigners live out in the suburbs. I got it [the apartment] through the grapevine. The landlady liked renting to foreigners 'cause she could raise rent each time renters moved out. Getting a chance to live there gave me a chance to see the medina firsthand.

Matt and his U.S. roommate reaped the reward of greater understanding of the Tunisian culture. Walking around the medina, chatting with shopkeepers, proved to be an education in itself.

> My roommate was good at buying textiles, so he would spend hours and hours haggling and buying textiles. It was neat to see what relationships were like.
>
> And to have *time*. There are great places to go in Minneapolis, but there's no time to go there. We always had arguments about this. I said that in the U.S. time is money and information is free. When you walk around the university, you see posters everywhere and signs—tons of information everywhere. We are bombarded. In Tunisia it seemed to be the reverse. Time was free, but information was money.
>
> In the bazaar, the information about how much something was worth was jealously guarded. I remember a film festival and there were no schedules available. I saw one schedule that someone had and I tried to find one, but it was impossible.

Matt reached this level of insight only by weathering some hard times. Lori, the Goshen College student, did not expect the cross-cultural experience to be so difficult and could not conquer the challenges she faced. Matt was fortunate because he knew that even frustrations could teach him valuable lessons.

> It was difficult just being away from home and friends. There were some difficult things like interactions with the bureaucracy. It just didn't work the way I wanted it to work. It was a lot slower.... That was hard.
>
> But there was a good aspect to it. It forced you

> to come out and fight for your rights. I didn't have a camera. My folks bought me a used one for forty or fifty dollars and sent it by mail to Tunisia. I got a message from the customs tax people saying the taxes were $150. Someone told me to take all my papers showing I was a student and to just go and beg. So I went, and I begged. I had to give my spiel to about ten different people, but it worked. "My mother is very old, and she didn't know you shouldn't do this. . . . " It was a hassle and I would rather not have had to do it, but it was OK.

The camera battle and many other situations helped Matt change and develop new attitudes toward the Middle East.

> It helps build your confidence a lot. When I first went to Morocco and Egypt, I didn't speak any Arabic. I felt it was really an intense place. It would be easy to feel threatened or vulnerable. And in Tunisia the same pressures were there, but I felt confident that I could live in a non-European, Third-World country, able to live with insects in the kitchen and not having heat and all that. So I feel that I could probably go to any Third-World country [now] and live.

Matt developed an understanding of the lives and struggles of Arabs.

> It made me aware of the Arab conflicts, Third-World, north-south conflicts. Since I've come back, I've really tried to read a lot and keep up and tried to read a lot about Tunisia too. Before I went, I was really curious about Tunisia, but now I really try to

> read everything, *Jeune Afrique,* even though the library doesn't carry some really important Middle East journals. Partly because Arabic . . . is not really much of a focus here.

Matt's efforts to build on his knowledge without much encouragement were not new. He had done the same in Tunisia, working to improve his Arabic. One of the factors that contributed most to his language development—traveling the countryside outside of Tunis—was not part of his institution's program. He did it on his own. As for the language instruction that was provided, Matt said "The Institute provided a good Arabic professor and a room for us to study, but apart from that . . . there wasn't a real feeling of community or anything."

Matt's comments reflected a loneliness that settles on students who excel in the study of foreign cultures and languages. He felt it most acutely when he returned to the United States.

> The university should consider what you did as having value—instead you come back from your overseas experience and the first thing that happens is that the financial aid office is after you. Not that they should have a welcoming committee, but just let the students know that what they have done is valued, is part of their education.

As they complete their university degrees, the returnees struggle with the decision of how—or if—they can incorporate their overseas experience as they plan their futures. As for Matt, he left on a positive note, full of plans.

> I want to continue to study Arabic. And my study of the medina really focused my interest in urban

geography, and not necessarily within the United States. And that would not have happened if I hadn't had the chance to go to Tunisia—an interest in the preservation of the medina, and an interest in research libraries. I'm intrigued by the Middle East, but I know I don't want to become a Middle East expert; there are enough of those. I'm thinking of public affairs, international affairs, and public planning.

CHAPTER TWO

INTELLECTUAL DEVELOPMENT ABROAD

Studies show that greater progress in the acquisition of a foreign language can be expected abroad than on the home campus. The amount of language learning increases with greater immersion into the foreign culture and less contact with other Americans. The amount of prior study of language correlates so poorly with the level of acquisition that it is an inadequate predictor of the ability of students to follow university courses abroad.

While abroad, many students are able to take courses in their majors that are not available on their home campuses.

Their perspectives on their majors may change, and they may discover additional career options related to their majors.

Students also show measurable increases in their knowledge of the foreign countries in which they study, including history, art, literature, and political systems. They also increase their interest in reflective thought, systematic thinking, and the value they place on familiarity with different schools of thought. These increases correlate as much with nonacademic pursuits abroad as they do with academic ones.

Finally, we discuss the problem faced by most programs in assessing the quality of courses taken abroad and assigning credit. We suggest several solutions.

Intellectual development is the principal goal of most academic programs abroad. The participants also experience living in another country and culture, but it is done while advancing their formal education by enrolling in a college or university program. Many students take advantage of these programs. According to *Open Doors 1968/87* (1988), nearly fifty thousand students annually receive academic credit for study outside the United States.

The experience of Robert, an Asian studies major at the University of California, Berkeley, offers insight into the sort of knowledge that can be better gained abroad than at home. Robert enrolled for his junior year at Beijing University under California's Education Abroad Program. The primary focus of that program is the study of modern Chinese; other courses about China are taught in English. Compared to the Chinese studies he undertook at Berkeley, his experience in China, where he could observe the culture firsthand, provided a much better understanding of the country.

> Before I went to China, I would read about things in a book. For instance, in political science I would study about Chinese politics, and we learned specific terms that described what was happening—how leaders took over and moved up in the ranks of politics. They would describe the connections involved with a Chinese word, *guan-xi*. So you would think, OK, guan-xi is how it works. But you go to China and you see that guan-xi pervades the whole society, that it is a really major issue, and that it also affects your own life. If you don't have guan-xi, then you suffer as a result. It means a lot more after you've gone there and you've seen it. You think, well, it's not just what you read in the book—it has meaning to you personally.

In this chapter we discuss three areas of intellectual growth which current research indicates are the most salient in the overseas study experience: foreign language learning; the expansion of learning in the major; and the increased general knowledge the student gains (which may be considered a broadening in general studies). We will also examine the challenge of measuring academic achievement and awarding academic credit for it.

LEARNING A FOREIGN LANGUAGE

Matt, the University of Minnesota student who went to Tunisia, studied Arabic and also used it for everyday communication. He believed his most valuable achievement in study abroad was his fluency in Arabic.

> The high point was getting a chance to study Arabic in an Arabic-speaking country. I had studied it here for about two and a half years. It was great to be living in that environment, where I could constantly be learning and listening to it. It was hard sometimes to make the shift from classical to Tunisian Arabic, especially at the beginning, but by the end I could switch and if I didn't know the word in Tunisian, I would be able to ask.

Matt believed he could learn a new language better in the country where it was spoken than he could from a book. Many students say that learning the language is their first priority in enrolling in study abroad programs, and many will continue to use their second language for advanced study and research.[1]

An important question then is what method of language study works best abroad? There is little research on the subject, which is not surprising. Research on language teaching methodologies in general is inadequate (Benzler and Schulz 1979, 59–70).[2] Foreign settings offer many new resources for instruction, practice, and evaluation. Teaching methods that take advantage of the local environments can certainly be expected to improve on the classroom methods used in the United States.

There have been two useful studies on language learning abroad. One is the Study Abroad Evaluation Project (SAEP) (Carlson et al. 1990). SAEP, a study conducted jointly by the European Institute of Education and Social Policy in Paris and four U.S. institutions, concluded that "most study abroad students [studying language in a foreign country] move from the intermediate to the advanced level in ... language proficiency" (52). SAEP tested students in French-, German-, and Swedish-speaking areas using two measurements. One was a self-appraisal method developed by the Educational Testing Service and the other a language proficiency oral interview developed by the American Council on the Teaching of Foreign Languages. These tested the four skills of speaking, listening comprehension, reading, and writing. The students became most proficient in speaking, listening, and reading, with writing skills lagging behind. SAEP cautions that there is no basis for the extrapolation of these data to non-European languages.

A study by Tracy Terrell (1982) of the University of California, Irvine, compared twenty-one students who participated for one quarter in a work and study program in Mexico with a group studying Spanish on the campus of the University of California, Irvine. The students in Mexico had taken a minimum of one year (three quarters) of Spanish at home and then took an additional quarter in Mexico. They were also, in their work and living experience, immersed in a Spanish-speaking culture. The control group in Irvine completed two full years (six quarters) of Spanish. Researchers then compared the groups' skills in speaking, listening comprehension, reading, and writing, using tests and taped interviews. The average speaking and listening comprehension score (83) of the students in Mexico exceeded the average score (75) of the students who had completed two years of Spanish on campus. The grammar and composition skills of the students in Mexico also proved equal to or better than those resulting from second-year courses at the UC campuses. Terrell attributed this to the Spanish language courses and written work required during the quarter in Mexico.[3]

Linguists and language teachers disagree on the amount of language instruction students need before going abroad. Some feel that at least two years of college instruction at home are required for students to make optimum progress.

Others argue that immersing students from the beginning in an environment where the language is spoken will give the optimum results. The Terrell study points out that "the score on the language exam correlated only weakly with the number of language courses taken on the UC campuses before entering the program" (9).

The SAEP study suggests that thorough immersion into the foreign society may be just as important for language development as prior study. One interesting finding of the study was that the more time a student spent with other Americans, the less the increase in language skills.

Few studies have tackled Asian or other languages considered especially difficult for English speakers.[4] However, researchers tend to agree that prior language study is a necessity with such languages. The question may be, however: just how much? Robert, the University of California student who went to China, makes this observation:

> Going to China with two years of college Chinese was enough—at least for me—to be able to get the basic things done. But then you get to the point where you want to understand nuances in the language and you learn differences in usage. This only comes from experience. You can't learn it in books. It comes with talking with people on the trains, reading newspapers, learning slogans, and things like that.

Some programs in Asian countries have found that even two years of prior study isn't enough, especially if the aim of the program is to provide academic training in subjects other than—or in addition to—language. Many program operators report that students going to Japan, China, or Korea with two years of language cannot follow regular university courses. For this reason, most programs in these countries offer either language classes on site, courses given in English, or some combination of the two. Many one-year programs report that with two years of prior language study plus language instruction on site, students are still only beginning to understand university lectures at the end of the year. This often prevents U.S. institutions from sending their students to the more prestigious institutions. Students may have to settle for a less prestigious institution that will arrange for the courses in English.

Prior language study is a must for some programs; for example, those designed for students to take courses in their majors or to carry out fieldwork abroad. Since the design, length, and approach of such programs vary widely, generalizing about them is difficult. One example is the year-long Massachusetts Institute of Technology program in Japan. The students' programs include time working as interns for businesses or institutions related to their majors. To function, they need a good working knowledge of Japanese before going.

Most colleges and universities have relied on the completion of a minimum language requirement at their institution as a measure of the students' skills. Yet, research like the Terrell study suggests that the amount of language study a student receives at home is not the best measure of competence abroad. Standardized tests of language proficiency are more accurate assessment tools.

Unfortunately, few are available. Other countries have only recently begun to devise language proficiency tests for university work similar to the Test of English as a Foreign Language (TOEFL) that is widely used in the United States to test incoming foreign students. France has decided to require a similar test, but only a few universities are currently using it. German universities give a test called the PNdS, but it is not standardized, and it varies in reliability depending on who constructs and corrects it. Swedish universities have had a proficiency requirement for some time.

There is an unpublished study, however, that throws some light on what might result from the administration of proficiency tests developed by foreign countries. The subject of the study, a program in Göttingen, Germany, required two years of German language study for admission and then put the students (fifty-eight of them) through five or six weeks of intensive language study on site before the program began. To determine whether the students were ready to follow courses in the target language, they were given the German PNdS examination. Forty-three percent of the students could not pass the test before taking the program's intensive in-country language course. Even after the five-week intensive course, 21 percent still had not reached the required minimum on the PNdS to begin regular course work and had to take further language work before enrolling in regular university courses.[5]

We are not aware of any U.S. universities administering these examinations as a part of student selection for study abroad. In fact, these examinations are apparently not even available in the United States. If they were, U.S. students who were going to enroll in regular courses at foreign institutions might be confronted with the same dilemma faced by foreign students, who must pass the TOEFL examination before being admitted to U.S. colleges and universities.

To date, colleges and universities have been reluctant to move to language competency testing (using tests prepared in the U.S.) as a part of student selection. This reluctance is due, in part, to the lack of a test that is both affordable and accurate. The tests devised by the American Council on the Teaching of Foreign Languages (ACTFL) are generally considered to adequately measure the skills required for foreign study, but most institutions deem them too costly because they must be administered by specially trained proctors. The tests of the Modern Language Association (MLAT) are relatively inexpensive to administer, but many people feel they do not adequately measure communication ability in the language. Furthermore, neither of these tests has been systematically correlated with a student's ability to perform in foreign universities.

From the research about language learning two things stand out. First, colleges and universities need to make major changes in the way they teach foreign languages. In particular, they need to find ways to carry out the instruction in locations where the language being learned is the dominant one in the surrounding culture.

Second, if students are being chosen to take courses offered in a foreign language in a university abroad, competency testing should be used in the selection process. It will probably cost more, but the low correlation of language skill with years of study means it is academically irresponsible to not ascertain whether the students have the competency to follow the courses.

GAINING A NEW PERSPECTIVE ON THE MAJOR

Karen, the California student who went to France, described how her year there helped her to choose a more specific direction for her major in foreign languages: "I always knew I wanted to do something with language . . . but I don't think I'm going to be a professor. It wasn't a change. It was just more of a focusing of what I can do with my language." Other students, like Matt, return home bursting with new ideas about where their majors can lead them. Even Lori, who was disappointed overall with her term abroad, gained confidence in her chosen field.

Students often take courses in their majors while abroad. The SAEP study (Carlson et al. 1990) found that 66 percent of the American students surveyed "took at least a few courses which they could not or would not have taken on their home campuses" (36). However, when asked to reflect on why study abroad was worthwhile, the students said that taking courses not offered at home was of secondary importance.

University and college planners rank the opportunity to take courses not offered on the home campus as an important academic goal. But, paradoxically, they often require a course name and number that reflects a course listed in some department on campus!

One problem relative to taking courses overseas which are credited toward the students' majors lies in assuring that the courses are of comparable quality to those at the home institution. One solution is offering courses at a location abroad but taught by home campus professors. For example, both the University of California and the Council on International Educational Exchange offer quarter-long courses in tropical biology in a Costa Rican rain forest. This provides an environment for fieldwork that cannot be duplicated in the U.S. The courses are taught in English, which circumvents the problem of teaching the students Spanish before they go but limits their interaction with the local culture.

In addition to specific courses in students' majors, often the entire experience of living in another culture broadens their perspectives on their fields of study. Margarita was a Goshen College art student who went to China. As part of her program she worked with a Chinese artist and had to wrestle with a different perspective on how one should learn to be an artist.

> Mr. Lee ... taught me a lot about water colors and how to do the animal and the whole concept of Chinese art, which is very different from the Western one. They are more concerned with the ideology and the concentration and we tend to be more concerned with the end product....

> Initially when I arrived, I thought their way of teaching art was very stifling because I put myself with my formal education in their position and said, "I could never stand this." For example, when you do a bird you take step one, you do the head first and then you end with the legs. I wanted to say "Well no, if you are going to be able to paint a bird, you should be able to do it like you want." It made me angry that the artists were so controlled in the creative aspect. But then I started to realize that it's a whole different perspective. I had to leave behind my concept of art to be able to understand theirs.

The new perspectives the students gain in their fields undoubtedly vary widely according to the culture of the country, the design of the program, and the predilections of the students themselves. Data are scarce on this subject. However, Billigmeier and Forman (1975, 223), in a study of students in a year abroad program in Germany, asked what the students thought the experience had given them that they might not have gotten at home. Eighteen percent indicated they had gained new perspectives in the content and methods of their major fields.

When these new vistas open up, students begin to see the career options for their majors more clearly. Before going abroad, Robert had worked for a company doing business with China and felt attracted to both business and to academia. When he was asked how his sojourn in China was changing his future plans, he said the following:

> Since I've been here, I have become interested in [researching] several issues and I probably have become more serious about going into academia, but I have serious reservations about it as being worthless and too haughty and an ivory tower type of

> thing. At the same time, I'm afraid of going into business because it seems to get very boring.... Originally, when I started studying Chinese, I thought I might be interested in going into business. Now that I've been in China, I realize what business in China really entails, and it's not as glossy as you read in the newspapers or as a lot of businessmen seem to think. And it's very complicated and takes a lot of time.

Like Robert, many students receive a good dose of realism about the nature of their chosen fields. Sometimes this causes them to narrow their choices, sometimes it opens their eyes to a world of new possibilities. Clayton went from the University of Minnesota to Kenya as part of his international development studies. After a field project involving photographic documentation of a low-cost, self-help housing project, his focus in international development changed.

> I learned that bottom-up, grass-roots development projects have had the shortest distances to fall should they fail, but the greatest chances for success because the people undertaking them are the potential benefactors. So I became inspired and thought, "This is what I want to do." And that's what I'm pursuing in my degree plan now—furthering information collection and making it available to grass-roots, self-help [groups].

INCREASING KNOWLEDGE IN GENERAL STUDIES

If students return home with new ideas about their majors, the impact on their attitudes and expectations toward learning in general is often even greater. Bob, a senior at the University of Minnesota, studied in Nice, France, under the auspices of the International Student Exchange Program. This program places the student directly into the foreign university. His reaction to the system of education is typical.

> It gave me an appreciation for what academia should be. I was convinced that the most important thing was to get the greatest number of credits and all A's, because that had always been my goal. But in France I started to think less about grades and began to be motivated by learning.

The SAEP study (Carlson et al. 1990, 131–32) found that after studying abroad, students considered getting good grades and learning facts less important goals than before. They had come to value systematic thinking, familiarity with different schools of thought, development of one's own point of view, and the acquisition of knowledge from different disciplines and from independent work.

One might assume that a deeper appreciation of academic learning would be directly related to involvement in a foreign educational institution, but the evidence does not seem to confirm this view. Instead, the experience of living and studying abroad in itself seems to awaken in young people the purposes of liberal education. The Goshen College students spend fourteen weeks in a program combining study and service, mainly in developing countries. Their study is arranged by the college and does not involve significant contact with a host country university. But one of the more surprising results of a study (Kauffmann and Kuh 1985) involving these students was the increase in their interest in reflective thought, a change which seemed to have persisted one year later.

If the academic experience of a student abroad is not

directed toward the major, it is best identified with the pursuit of a liberal education. The coursework might be aimed simply at expanding the student's view of the world, or it might be part of a specialized general studies curriculum required by the home campus. Study abroad students and their universities are thus drawn into a national debate over the meaning of "liberal education." Is it a course of study directed toward developing the person into something that can be called "educated"? Is it a checklist of courses which assures us that the student knows a certain minimum of information and possesses a given level of skills in writing, mathematics, and foreign language? Goodwin and Nacht (1988, 6) ask:

> Can it be defined as the mastery of a set of subjects and courses, or does it involve above all personal growth of the students? If the latter, can such qualities as personal maturity and sensitivity, extension of perspective, and appreciation and tolerance of difference, be identified and measured? And if they can indeed be measured ... should college "credit" be awarded for their acquisition?

We suggest in chapter 5 that cognitive development and personal growth are inextricably intertwined. Study in a foreign culture brings into play forces which affect personal growth but which also stimulate and enhance cognitive learn eing. We believe that this is part of the reason that the SAEP study (Carlson et al. 1990, 3) found that students gained the most from two disparate, almost contradictory, aspects of the year abroad: their nonacademic pursuits on the one hand and the intellectual experience on the other.

Don was not pursuing courses in his major when he studied in Costa Rica. The entire trimester abroad was designed as a part of the formal general education program at

Goshen College. He believed that personal changes were the most important result of his experience. However, his personal development also had a direct impact on his academic achievements. New horizons in learning opened to him. He was motivated to continue the study of Spanish, and the trimester after his return, he received A's in all his classes for the first time in his college career.

The SAEP study (Carlson et al. 1990, 155) also found that the students' levels of knowledge about their host countries increased dramatically as a result of having lived and studied there. Karen's program leaders in France encouraged her to nurture an interest in intellectual and artistic activities. She took a course in art history. She visited museums and attended concerts, plays, and lectures, both in Poitiers and during frequent weekend trips to Paris. French friends and acquaintances were more interested in the arts than her companions at home had been. And her environment was replete with opportunities.

The SAEP study (Carlson et al. 1990, 36) reported that 68 percent of their students in Western Europe took courses to broaden themselves culturally. Such courses are available at most host universities. Thirty-one percent of the students in the Billigmeier and Forman study (1975, 225), for instance, said that exposure to art, architecture, literature, music, and theater in Germany was a major element of their overseas experience.

American institutions also develop special courses to take advantage of the rich cultural environment in Europe. They use the museums and art galleries of Paris, Rome, Florence, Berlin, Barcelona, Athens, and many other cities as integral parts of courses designed especially for U.S. students. For example, in Madrid several institutions offer art courses using the Prado as the locus; courses in London are built around the plays that are currently running.

A plethora of short courses "on location" appear in college summer or interterm catalogues. Typically, the professors take groups abroad for intensive, highly focused study using the rich resources at hand. Examples include the study of art in Italy, architecture in Denmark, the classics in Greece, music in Austria, theater in Great Britain, and poetry in Ireland.

Of course, such studies are not limited to Western civilization. American students are becoming literate in the arts in other traditions and cultures. We've described how Margarita began to understand Chinese art differently after living and working with an artist in Chengdu. She called the experience "a window on the culture" that allowed her to see China from a different perspective. Others have studied archeology in Mexico, Togo, and Morocco. Dance, puppetry, and the gamelan have been part of programs in Indonesia and Thailand.

To date no systematic research has compared the effectiveness of on-site cultural studies to classroom work in the same subjects in the United States. However, educators generally agree that students learn better by studying the arts in their original setting.

THE QUALITY OF FOREIGN COURSES AND THE PROBLEM OF CREDIT

We have already alluded to the problem universities face of making sure that the quality of courses given abroad measures up to the standards of the home campus. The research studies in this area suffer from several problems. First, quality is a difficult concept to pin down, and educators have not been able to agree upon a working definition. A. W. Astin (1987, 12) observes, "*Excellence* and *quality* are the fashionable terms in discussing education these days. But even as we talk about excellence, we seldom define what we mean by it. It's here that our implicit values come into play."[6]

Even if there were an accepted definition of quality, we lack adequate instruments to measure it across cultural boundaries. Objective tests now in use simply examine the knowledge gained in particular courses. For example, the American Chemical Society has standardized tests that cover courses in analytical, physical, and organic chemistry. But such standardized examinations are carefully constructed to measure specific desired outcomes for the United States. The goals of a course in a foreign university, even if they are similarly stated, are likely to be different.

For this reason, most studies of relative academic quality rely on participant perceptions. This approach suffers from at least two obvious weaknesses. The students are not likely to have had the same courses at home; otherwise, they would not be taking them abroad. Further, most students, even after a year of study in a foreign university, do not adequately grasp the fundamental differences in the two systems of education. They still evaluate the courses abroad in terms of teaching methods at home.

These caveats notwithstanding, the SAEP study (Carlson et al. 1990, 36–37) asked 301 students from different U.S. institutions to compare the quality of the academic programs in the universities abroad with their home campus courses. Using a scale with a low of 1 and a high of 5 (the mean being 3.0), students ranked their perceptions of the academic standards expected of American students as being lower in Germany (2.25) and France (2.37) and about the same in Sweden (3.0) and the United Kingdom (3.03).

While there are no concrete data available, the conventional wisdom in the field, based on returned students' questionnaires and comments, is that the quality of academic programs in southern Europe, Japan, and most if not all Third-World countries is perceived to be lower than in the U.S. Of course, in comparing specific institutions, students rank some courses as superior.

A noteworthy observation of the SAEP study was that students rated their general intellectual development during their time abroad as higher (3.72 on a scale of 1–5) than it would have been had they stayed at home. Among European nations, the U.K. ranked the highest in this regard (3.96) and France the lowest (3.59). The students ranked their home institutions higher than foreign ones when it came to organization of lectures and classes and the use of frequent assignments and evaluations. These are obviously culturally dependent issues. Ironically, the students also criticized their home institutions for not treating them as mature, independent learners and for requiring them to work under the artificial pressure of external rewards, such as grades.

Evaluating quality is only part of the larger task of assigning credit for academic work done abroad. The unit of credit, as a measure of academic performance, is unique to American higher education; therefore, universities need to translate the foreign courses into credit units to integrate the learning of U.S. students abroad into the home university. A study done for the American Association of College Registrars (Krawutschke 1980, 33–34) concluded that 94 percent of U.S. institutions must deal with the question of what credit to give for study abroad. Many smaller institutions rely on the advice of nearby larger universities in assigning credit.

A variety of schemes have been used. If the courses abroad are taught exclusively for U.S. students, the professor can follow an American system of grading. Even that can present problems, however, especially when the course is taught by a foreign teacher who is unfamiliar with the grading system used in the home university. Attempts by such instructors to assign grades in an unfamiliar system often bring complaints of unfairness from students. Where relatively small numbers of students are involved, professors at the home institution are sometimes asked to evaluate the papers and examinations, or to test the students after they return, and to assign credits and grades for courses taken abroad. Some schools simply assign a given number of credit hours to study abroad and record it without grades. Other programs treat the courses as independent studies, which are evaluated by home professors as such.

Institutions that send abroad resident directors from the U.S. rely on them to assign the grades. They must collect the evaluations, or semester or yearly grades, from the host university teachers and translate them into the U.S. system.

The University of California has been using this approach to assigning credits and grades for years, while allowing researchers to track the grade point averages (GPA) of students in the Education Abroad Program. For the seventeen-year period beginning with 1962–63, there were 5,676 students who went abroad in this program. The average GPA before departure was 3.30 based on a maximum of 4.0. During their studies abroad, they had an overall GPA of 3.48, which dropped to 3.37 after their return. There was no control group; however, examination of student performances on one of the campuses leads one to believe that this increase in GPA while abroad was greater than it would have been had the students remained on the home campus.

Students do need to be held accountable for their progress, but in the final analysis it is also important to recognize that the genius of study abroad is that it allows students a new system of education, a new approach to learning, a new set of stimuli for intellectual achievement and personal development, and new criteria for success.

The task of determining the quality of foreign courses and assigning credit may always be problematic. This in itself is symbolic of the wildly divergent intellectual riches awaiting eager young minds all over the world. Research has begun to confirm what students and their institutions have believed all along: that language learning is better abroad, that courses and viewpoints not available at home can enrich major studies, and that short, on-site courses as well as longer-term exposure to a different educational tradition can greatly expand academic horizons. To force the experience into the mold of the home college or university too rigidly would defeat the purpose.

NOTES

1. See Carlson and Yachimowicz (1987); Prater, Barrutia, Larkin, and Weaver (1980); Koester (1987); and Billigmeier and Forman (1975).

   Students who listed development of foreign language skills as their first priority in going abroad made up the majority in the University of California studies. In the Koester study, students who bought identity cards listed improvement in a foreign language as their third-ranked goal.

   Six years after returning home from a year-long program in Germany, 38 percent of the students in the Billigmeier and Forman study indicated that they had used their skills in German for advanced study and research.

2. One must agree with Hosenfeld's (1979, 51) assessment that "a review of current research in foreign language education reveals a plethora of studies marred by inadequate problem development, lack of control of extraneous variables, invalid criterion measures, and inappropriate statistical techniques."

   Benzler and Schulz conclude that there is no clear empirical evidence that one method is superior to another in terms of student achievement, with the possible exception of intensive instruction.

3. Tracy Terrell carried out an examination of Spanish language learning as a part of an evaluation of the University of California program involving a study and work program in Mexico. The evaluation committee consisted of Thomas J. LaBelle (Chair), Nicholas Royal, and Tracy Terrell. The unpublished report was submitted in 1982 under the name "SAW Program in Mexico" and is available from the Education Abroad Program systemwide office, University of California, Santa Barbara, CA 93106.

4. So far the study by Kim (1988) has involved two groups of UCLA students who spent one quarter in Korea. The small number of students involved, the range of language skills which the students brought to the program, and the lack of an appropriate comparison group has precluded definitive conclusions.

5. From an unpublished study of University of California students at Göttingen during the 1987–88 year.

6. Astin argues that we tend to look at excellence either in terms of the reputation of the institutions or in terms of their resources. He suggests a better approach would be "their ability to develop the talents of students."

CHAPTER THREE

DEVELOPING AN INTERNATIONAL PERSPECTIVE

In this chapter we discuss how study abroad influences the students' development of an international perspective. Specifically, they show changes in three aspects: in their perceptions of host and home cultures and in their global understanding.

Students are more likely to develop favorable attitudes toward the host country if they (1) start out with realistic expectations about it, (2) spend a significant amount of time there (six months or more), and (3) experience a high degree of immersion in the culture.

Changes in students' attitudes toward their home culture are apparently conversely related to the attitudes developed toward the host culture. An increased appreciation of the host culture is sometimes accompanied by more critical views of the home country. That happens when new values, attitudes, and ideas adopted from the host country seem in direct conflict with those encountered by the students back home in the United States.

Most research on the development of global perspectives—or global understanding—by study abroad students focuses on knowledge acquisition, behavioral change, or affective change. Only a few studies explore the first two, however. In contrast, there is considerable research on affective change, though the methodologies are diverse and the findings contradictory. All three are reviewed in this chapter.

In addition to the more traditional academic outcomes of improved foreign language proficiency, increased knowledge in one's discipline, and a broadened intellectual perspective, an educational experience abroad is purported to endow students with an international perspective—knowledge, attitudes and skills which presumably lead to a better educated citizenry and ultimately to improved international relations and global understanding.

Goodwin and Nacht (1988, 12) describe this rather amorphous goal.

> The defenders of this goal speak especially of a personal metamorphosis in those who partake—a ge-

> stalt change that varies with the individual, cannot be predicted in detail, but is enormously important as an outcome. Students in this way become, it is said, more mature, sophisticated, hungry for knowledge, culturally aware, and sensitive. They learn by questioning their prejudices and all national stereotypes. They ask the meaning of national culture. Their horizons are extended and they gain new perspectives.

While many would agree that these are desirable goals for an educated person in today's shrinking world, researchers have not reached consensus on what is meant by an international perspective, or how it can be measured. And yet when asked, returned students as well as administrators of study abroad programs vigorously assert that acquiring this perspective is one outcome of an experience abroad. This conviction is reflected in comments from returned students.

> Now I really see the interdependence and have a lot more respect for other cultures, and I see that humanity really does have something universal that links us together.

> I feel more globally involved. I read the national headlines first, then I go right to the world headlines and read everything.

> I have a better understanding of foreign students and a better understanding of the Arab side of the political conflict.

> I learned the other side, the Tamil "terrorists'" view. And it made me realize that they do have a reason to fight. Now I can look at any situation

> where people are labeled "terrorists" and "guerrillas" and I realize there has to be a reason that they're fighting.

In this chapter we summarize research to date in three areas that help to define international perspective: changes in students' perception and understanding of the host culture and of the home culture, and the development of global understanding. Research results in the first two areas are relatively consistent and easily interpreted; research measuring changes in global understanding has been less clear conceptually and has yielded conflicting results.

CHANGES IN PERCEPTION OF HOST COUNTRY

One of the most frequently touted objectives of study abroad programs is to create more positive attitudes toward peoples of other cultures. It is assumed that if individuals are simply given the opportunity to interact, mutual understanding and positive attitudes will ensue. However, a large body of literature in social psychology suggests that cross-cultural contact leads to favorable attitude changes only if certain conditions are met (Allport 1954; Amir 1969, 319–43; Brislin 1981, 171–200; Gudykunst 1979, 1–16). For example, people are more likely to feel favorable toward another group if they interact with members of the other group in a supportive environment and if there is opportunity to go beyond superficial interaction. Intercultural contact is less likely to result in positive attitude change if these two conditions are not met.

Research on the outcomes of study abroad generally confirms these findings. Like other travelers, students will develop more favorable attitudes toward their host cultures under certain conditions (Sell 1983, 131–47). These conditions include preexisting attitude, duration of stay, and the degree to which the student is immersed in the host culture. The location may also play a role—Austria, for instance, tends to elicit positive responses from students, France more negative—but the research evidence is shaky on this point. Therefore, while we discuss this issue, we do not consider it a primary factor.

Krista and Bob offer interesting contrasts relative to these factors. They both had recently participated in University of Minnesota study abroad programs in Europe. Krista, a junior who changed her major from biology to international agriculture after going abroad, spent a semester in Graz, Austria. Bob, a senior majoring in English, had studied for a year in Nice, France.

While both students enjoyed their study abroad and felt that they gained a lot from the experience, Krista returned with a more positive attitude toward Austria and Austrians and a more critical view of the United States. Bob, on the other hand, returned with a renewed appreciation for the United States and a more negative feeling about France.

One aspect of Austrian life that Krista came to appreciate over time was the pattern of friendships. While it took longer initially to get to know people well, her relationships with Austrian friends seemed deeper than her friendships in the States.

> When I first went to Austria, I thought that Austrians were cold, really stoic. And now that I'm here I think that Americans are cold and Austrians are warm. I think Americans are superficial, too.

She also reported positive attitudes toward the Austrian educational system.

> I was really surprised at how they [university students] are committed to learning. I spent some time in a kindergarten class, and we studied the whole education system, and I just think that before Austrians get into university, they have a more well-rounded education.... Being well-rounded before you get into university is important because it helps you understand what your options are.

In contrast, Bob became somewhat critical of French culture.

> It's kind of—to me—a tense culture, real rigid. You have to do the right thing, wear the right clothes and that kind of thing. I found that frustrating.

He felt the French attitudes toward women were "really disconcerting," that "the sexism there is really bad," and that "it was hard to be male there sometimes." He was also surprised at attitudes toward art in France.

> I thought [before studying there] that French people were more in tune to art. And I think that's true, but one of the things I noticed was that they didn't seem to enjoy that awareness, but felt pressure to know about it. It's a real pedantic orientation. They didn't know it to enjoy it, they knew it to show they knew it.

He illustrated this with an experience he had at a party in Paris. He struck up a conversation with a German and a French student. The German was doing his thesis on a church outside Paris, and the French student was appalled and apologetic because he had never heard of this church. As Bob reported it: "He went on and on and couldn't drop it and was so aghast, and so embarrassed. And I just thought, 'What fun is that? It's a nice church, would be something nice to go see next weekend.' "

Bob, like Krista, was favorably impressed with the educational system in his host country. "Their system is ... oriented toward the way universities started out to be—you want to learn about the stars, you go talk to this guy." But he was critical as well: "It was also limiting. If you are a history major, you have three electives your whole career and the rest is history. It was strange. Their universities are a little behind ours."[1]

It is easy to see how Bob and Krista developed different perceptions of their host countries. Let's examine how these differences relate to those aspects of the overseas study experience we mentioned earlier which affect the development of positive or negative perceptions of the host culture: preexisting attitudes, length of stay, the degree of immersion, and location.

PREEXISTING ATTITUDES AND EXPECTATIONS

In addition to being well immersed in the culture and spending an adequate time in Austria, Krista also had positive and realistic expectations prior to beginning her study abroad. She had already met the son of her host family when he came to visit her hometown, had talked at length with her friend who had lived with the same host family on the same program the year before, and had felt generally positive about going abroad.[2]

She developed realistic expectations concerning her study abroad in Austria. She enrolled in a foreign studies minor, available to any study abroad student at her university. The foreign studies minor was designed to complement any major and comprised a core of language, area studies, and intercultural communication offered in predeparture and reentry courses. While the predeparture class helped her understand Austrians better, there were still surprises. "What I learned about Austrians held true for the family. They *were* more formal and it was good to know that. But I wasn't at all prepared for the students. I expected *them* to be more formal."

Bob reported that his expectations for his year in France were quite unrealistic. "When I envisioned my year in Nice . . . I had all the daydreams and fantasies that go along with going to the French Riviera for a year. I guess I was ill prepared from that point of view." He spoke at length about his visions of meeting and falling in love with a rich woman from Monaco, who would support him while he wrote great literature, inspired by his life in the south of France!

Unlike Krista, he was not very knowledgeable about French culture, even though he had taken French and written papers about French culture. He now sees that he "had no idea what French culture was like" and resents those writing assignments where he had to compare American and French culture. "I realize I had no basis for comparison." He also found that his French language skills were not sufficient for him to succeed in the academic courses. He ended up auditing courses and received no academic credit for his study abroad.

Length of Stay[3]

Krista spent about six months in Austria, which seems to be the minimum amount of time needed to produce meaningful outcomes for the study abroad student. Even though Bob spent more time, the barriers he experienced in getting into the culture probably served to reduce the value of the longer stay.

Early researchers discovered that when students stay abroad for only a short time, they experience minimal impact and few personal changes.[4] They often do not have the time to develop relationships with people in the host country or to enter into the host culture to any significant degree. Beth, for example, took a short trip to Israel as a high school student but said she didn't see the "real" Israel. "I could have been anywhere in the world." She came back with a stereotype of Israelis as pushy and aggressive, especially compared to people in the Midwest where she had lived for most of her life. Clayton, who spent three months in an internship in Kenya, talked about his lack of assimilation in such a short visit, being "constantly aware that I was the foreigner." He felt the impact of the experience was minimal: "I didn't change myself, my personality, even the things I said about my own country or any other. I didn't feel a need to change."

Recent research sponsored by the Council on International Education Exchange (CIEE) suggests an optimal length of stay may be six to twelve months. In this research, Jolene Koester (1985; 1987) found that, all other things being equal, students who were abroad for more than six months but no more than twelve reported the greatest impact.[5] However, a report of an experimental program conducted by Sikkema and Niyekawa (1987) suggests that if carefully designed and accompanied by effective predeparture and postreturn academic coursework, a sojourn of two or three months can have an impact as great as, if not greater—at least in the grasp of the principles of cross-cultural interaction and intercultural learning—than much longer programs.[6]

IMMERSION IN THE HOST CULTURE[7]

While Krista's study abroad program could be described as an "island program," in which she took courses only with other American students, she took advantage of opportunities to become integrated into Austrian society. She lived with a host family and joined a local student volleyball team. She also reported that it was easier to get to know Austrians where she lived—in Graz—than in other cities, like Vienna, where there were many more American students.

She reported that living with a family was "great, because I really got to meet Austrians, and I was forced to use my German. It was fantastic." She spoke enthusiastically about the experience of living with her host family. The two sons were about her age, eighteen and twenty, and the daughter was thirteen. She did many things with the oldest boy and some with the younger son. Both boys were just entering their first year at the university, so they all shared the experience of being new on campus.

She shared a lot of activities with her family—hiking in the mountains, traveling to other Austrian cities, and going shopping on Saturdays. With the mother, she exchanged needlework and watched a daily soap opera. She remarked that what was meaningful about her interactions with her host family was "not any one big thing; it was just the time I spent with them."

At the end of her stay in Austria she felt well accepted by her family.

> At first I was "Krista, the American," then I was "Kris, the American," and by the end I was "Kris, the daughter." Two weeks before I left, the father came up and said, "You're my kid." That was neat, and it made me feel really good.

Living with a host family often provides the kind of experiences that help students assimilate into the foreign culture and see the culture from the inside. Youth exchange organizations like AFS International/Intercultural Programs and Youth For Understanding (YFU), which place high school students in host families all over the world, attest to the impact of this kind of experience (Hansel 1986). Students we interviewed often mentioned their host families as the most important factor in helping them integrate into the culture.

For example, LeeAnn, a junior in speech communication, spent a year in Sri Lanka with AFS just before entering college. She said that the best part of her experience by far was her family. She felt a rapport from the very beginning that she attributed to the fact that they were liberal, were of Dutch-Sinhalese descent, and spoke English. But she also felt it was easy to communicate with them because "they were anxious to know how I felt . . . that's what really helped my transition the most—our communication, from the first time when they had to show me how to use the bathroom."

Like Krista, LeeAnn found that it was the daily activities and interactions with the family that developed a bond, a rapport that can ultimately lead to insights about the people and culture of the host country. She said she didn't associate much with others because the family unit in Sri Lanka was so strong.

> Everyone would get home around five, and the TV didn't come on until six or seven, so we'd just sit around for hours and talk and talk, and they'd ask me to say something and we'd talk about cultural differences . . . and we'd play cards, and I'd just sit at home.

During the day, she helped with the laundry, "washing clothes at the well, squatting," helped the maid scrape coconuts, and sometimes helped her host mother with a daycare she maintained for local families.

Another way students can immerse themselves in the culture is by participating in extracurricular activities. Krista, for example, enrolled in a university volleyball course. The teacher didn't speak any English, so she had to speak German, and it gave her the opportunity to interact directly with her peers. Through volleyball, she got an idea of what student life was like and had fun. "The volleyball team understood me right away, and accepted me. There weren't many women who played, and I played a lot. I still keep in touch with them and they're bugging me to come back, and I'd love to." As with the family, the contact with the volleyball team afforded her an opportunity for more than superficial interaction; it provided another way of sharing aspects of daily life in the host country.

In contrast to Krista and LeeAnn, Bob had problems assimilating into the French culture, especially the student culture at the University of Nice. His French was not very good. He found that getting to know French students was hard, partly because they were so used to Americans; there was no novelty in being American. He felt he wasn't taken seriously. "I was just one of the Americans. . . . They've seen enough Americans come and go, that they aren't willing to . . . make a friend who's going to leave, just like last year and the year before." Also, he found that French students tended to socialize in groups, making it hard for him to get to know individual students.

He complained about the American students who didn't want to be in France: "They whined excessively and made sweeping generalizations about French people and French men. . . . It was hard to have them around sometimes." Nonetheless, he found it easier to make friends with them than with French students. At times he got tired of speaking French and would pull back into the American group a little. "It [speaking French] was real tiring—like being in class all day." He tried to gravitate toward those who were also making an effort to become friends with French as well as other foreign students. In the end he counted those American friends as one of the most positive aspects of his year abroad.

Location of Study Abroad

Research results also suggest that *where* students study may contribute to their positive or negative attitudes about their host countries, though at present the research is inconclusive and, indeed, has produced conflicting results.[8] While students in England and Austria have been found in these studies to have consistently come away with positive impressions and students in France with negative ones, both West Germany and Italy appear on both sides of the ledger. Further, in one study, Switzerland, Spain, and the USSR appear on the negative side, a finding which almost certainly needs to be tested with further research.

The reasons for students' consistently low ratings of France are not yet clear. There is evidence suggesting that foreign students in general—not just Americans—are less satisfied with their academic pursuits in France and, not coincidentally, with their degree of contact with host nationals than are students in other countries. This research is inconclusive, and it has not yet addressed the question of why these impressions form as they do. Klineburg and Hull (1979, 50–66) suggest that the problem may not lie in the location of the study abroad program per se but in the opportunity (or lack of it) for students to integrate themselves into the local culture.[9] In countries outside Western Europe, the reasons why students have less contact with their hosts are more readily apparent. Often prevailing societal or religious norms preclude meaningful, in-depth interactions. For example, students in Islamic countries sometimes find it difficult to achieve more than superficial relationships with the host nationals.

Like Matt, Sue spent a year in Tunisia at the Bourghiba Institute on a scholarship. These two students were successful in many ways in finding a niche in that society. Both had the requisite language skills (Matt knew Arabic, Sue knew

French), were directly enrolled in the foreign institution, spent little time with other American students, and stayed the optimum length of time. Both sought out opportunities to get to know Tunisians, and both found it difficult.

As Matt described it:

> I wouldn't say I was ever immersed in Tunisian culture, though I certainly was more than most students because of living in the medina. But it was really difficult because I'm not a Muslim. It was really hard for some people to accept me into their families when I wasn't a Muslim. It was hard for me to meet Tunisian women.
>
> It was difficult to get to know Tunisians.... If I wanted to talk about in-depth things, like traditional Muslim religion, and I'm sure Tunisians talk about that, they wouldn't with me, a foreigner.

As noted before, research investigating the relationship between location of study abroad and perceptions of the host country provides insufficient data from which to draw conclusions and, in being limited to Western Europe, offers us little on the experiences of students going to non-Western countries.

CHANGE IN PERCEPTIONS OF THE HOME CULTURE

Peter Adler, a social psychologist whose seminal work on culture learning is often cited, suggests that the journey abroad begins as a journey into another culture but ultimately becomes a journey of enhanced awareness and understanding of oneself (1975, 13–23). Stated differently, exposure to another culture and to other ways of thinking and behaving leads to new ways of looking at one's own culture. For most students, study abroad is a unique opportunity to compare firsthand various forms of government, systems of education, values, and lifestyles. This opportunity for comparison may result in a changed perception of one's home country, leading to more critical attitudes, more positive attitudes, or both. There is some evidence to suggest that attitudes toward the host culture and home culture may be conversely related; increased appreciation for the host culture is usually accompanied by more critical views toward one's own culture and vice versa (Carlson and Widaman 1988, 14; Carlson and Jensen 1984; Carlson and Yachimowicz 1985; Klineburg and Hull 1979; Marion 1980; Kafka 1968).

Again, Krista and Bob serve as good examples of students whose attitudes toward their home culture changed. Krista grew more critical of the United States as a result of her study abroad, while Bob became more positive. Nevertheless, Bob's changes in attitude did not reflect a clear-cut inverse relationship. He maintained some criticisms of his home country and some praise for his host country. Research studies show that student perceptions about the home and host culture often alter in both negative and positive directions. Overall, Bob's experience in France led to a new appreciation of certain American values.

> I became less anti-American. Before going to France, I thought we were a nation without morals. I really hated our foreign policy in the last eight years and that's part of it too. Capitalism seems bad, but there's a certain American spirit that comes through. It isn't always good, but it's *there*. There's something about Americans that's creative, and a certain lightness in spirit that I associate with Africans. So I realized that I like being American, I like America.... And that was a real surprise.

Students like Bob who return with a renewed overall appreciation for the United States often fit the same profile of those who were also more critical of the host culture: they have not integrated very well into the culture, have fewer host friends and more American friends, are more inflexible and conservative to begin with (determined through predeparture tests), and are less proficient in the host culture language (Marion 1980).

In contrast to Bob's attitudes, the criticisms of the many students who develop more negative attitudes toward the United States often center on perceived social and political apathy, on the American lifestyle and values, and on the government's foreign policy. Our interviews with returned students reflected these opinions. They compared U.S. citizens to people in other countries and observed that we rarely concern ourselves with political or social issues unless they touch us personally. For example, Krista observed that people in the United States were not very interested in a topic that was of utmost importance in Austria.

> It was interesting because Austrians thought that Americans were in favor of banning Waldheim from entering the States, and I think that most Americans don't even know about Waldheim. I know so many Americans who don't care, who aren't aware of what our country's doing.

Beth reported that she too was struck by the apathy of her American friends.

> I came back from Israel during the Iran-Contra hearings and I had no idea what was going on. My excuse was that I had been abroad, but the rest of these people had no excuse—it was basic ignorance. They didn't care. I never realized how little people care here. So that was a real shock.

This new look at life in the United States is probably a result of living in countries where people are more intensely affected by politics, where they are more involved in local social and political issues, and where the subject of politics is a frequent topic of conversation.

Krista also noted the difference between student involvement in Austria and student apathy in the United States.

> I am really involved in student government here, and it's like pulling teeth trying to get students involved. In Austria, the government cut some of the students' financial aid and they went on strike. There were hundreds of students at these rallies, protesting. It was very political and the three main parties were represented. It made an impression on me and showed me how uninterested Americans are in politics.

Sue said,

> Tunisians would want to know what I thought about Reagan or whatever American intervention was going on at the time. And I just didn't have any idea. I was not very political. But they expect you to be, and it's not acceptable for a Tunisian to not be political. Everyone has an opinion about what's happening. And here in the States, hardly *anybody* has an opinion, and that's the way it's supposed to be. Somebody said that people going abroad in an election year had better know everything that's going on in the election or else they'll feel really stupid. No matter who gets elected, they're going to have to justify it to their acquaintances abroad.

Much of the criticism reflects the students' conflict between the new values, attitudes, and ideas they may have adopted from the host country and what they see on their return to the United States. This seems to be particularly true for college students who have not yet solidified their own beliefs and values and, through exposure to the foreign culture, have adopted new ways of thinking and behaving (Gullahorn and Gullahorn 1963, 33–47). We will discuss this further in the next chapter.

Krista found that her relationships with Austrians made her more critical of certain aspects of her friendships in the U.S.

> I'm more critical of the U.S.... There, seeing the process I had to go through to earn their friendship ... like with the volleyball team—at the end, I was really close to them. It was an affectionate relationship; there was a lot of hugging. It was more of a group feeling. There are times that I can do that with people who aren't really close to me, but people I'm closer to would be uncomfortable if I did it. I think, if it seems appropriate in the situation, let's do it and let's not worry about being embarrassed or whatever.

She also found that in contrast to Austrians, Americans seem to always be in a hurry.

> The other thing about Americans is that everything is too rush, rush, rush. We need to slow down.... My lifestyle is much slower now. I spend a lot more time with just me, and it's neat, something that I didn't do before.

Like Krista, Sue also returned with a new appreciation for taking time to develop relationships and to savor the moment. However, she was more critical of the United States overall. While not completely positive in her attitudes toward her host country, Tunisia, her experience there seemed to lead to a rejection of many mainstream U.S. values.

> I have a really hard time accepting America, in terms of what it stands for and what it means to me for the future. In terms of living here and staying here—I can't see myself growing old in this country. I can't see myself working for any length of time in any of the respected institutions, like the big corporations.... There has to be a place where I like the way they do things!

While early researchers simply asked students to indicate a generalized positive or negative perception, students were asked in a recent study to specify the areas in which they felt more positive and negative about the United States. Their responses revealed that students felt slightly more positive about postsecondary or higher education; treatment of recently arrived immigrant groups; television, radio, newspapers, magazines; and customs and traditions. At the same time, students reported that they felt more negative about U.S. foreign policy and American cultural life (art, music, theater, literature). There was no change in students' opinions about the social structure (family, class system) in the United States (Carlson et al. 1990).

Carlson and Widaman (1988, 1–17) observe that "the sojourn seems to result in more mature and objective perceptions of the students' home country." Bob's reflections illustrate this point succinctly.

> My worldview changed a lot. There's still a lot that I don't like about America, but ... with that appreciation there also has come a sense of responsibility, since we are one of the few countries in a position to take the world in a different direction.

For many students, then, these changing attitudes toward the United States—whether positive or negative or both—are simply part of a more informed view of the world. The study abroad experience has led them to a new appreciation of their country as well as criticism of certain aspects of the American way of life (Koester 1985; Martin 1987, 337–56).

GLOBAL UNDERSTANDING

In this chapter we define global understanding as an awareness of, interest in, and concern for international events and issues. Research measuring change in students' global understanding is difficult to summarize, since the concept has been measured in a variety of ways. Our review of the literature and our own experience in international education leads us to believe that this aspect of developing an international perspective is complex and difficult to treat in a traditional reductionistic manner. Our interviews with students reinforced this position, as we pushed them to differentiate among the variables identified in the literature (changes in worldview, political concern, world-mindedness). A quote from a thoughtful graduate student, Gayle, who studied in both Spain and Germany, reflects this inability to reduce these changes to discrete entities.

> I experienced a change in self-awareness and a change in the way I approach learning.... I was

> starting to observe the world from a different angle and I couldn't really figure it out.... It's a very philosophical approach and deeply rooted in self-awareness. At the same time I can extrapolate it to the world. I would say that my worldview has definitely grown and been enhanced, but at the same time it's an introspective phenomenon. It's a journey outward, but also a journey inward.... It's difficult to describe because I can't separate the self-awareness from the global awareness.

However, insisting upon a holistic, nonreductionist approach limits our understanding of the contributions of previous research. Therefore, we identify three broad but distinct dimensions of global understanding: knowledge acquisition, affective change, and changes in behavior. A review of the literature reveals that most measures of change in global understanding fit into one of these three categories.

Knowledge acquisition includes measures of increased awareness and acquisition of facts concerning international affairs. Research investigating affective changes deals primarily with interest in international issues and world-mindedness as well as the ability to take the viewpoint of another cultural group (empathy). Finally, changes in behavior are measured by actions which reflect increased knowledge and affective changes, like participation in events and activities that are internationally oriented.

The same factors that influence changes in perception of host and home cultures come into play here also. In addition, another factor may be important: previous experience abroad. Based on the research and our interviews with study abroad students, we suggest that a first cross-cultural experience is more likely to produce personal growth than to increase in-depth cultural and global understanding. During a first trip abroad, a student primarily matures, expands horizons, learns to be more independent and self-reliant, and acquires survival skills for coping with new environments. In subsequent intercultural experiences, the student can concentrate on building cultural and global understanding.

A number of students attested to this developmental sequence. Sue, who had traveled in Europe before her year in Tunisia, said that her first experience abroad gave her self-confidence. "What Europe showed me was that I could do all the mechanical things like find a place to stay, that I wouldn't starve, and that I could read a train schedule." In Tunisia she acquired more insights about herself and the realities of life in the Arab world. Now, she's looking forward to another international experience, maybe with the Peace Corps.

> I know I can build on what I've learned. Just being in Tunisia and traveling in Europe—I learned more in those fifteen months than I've learned in my whole life. So if I could have two years or more of a situation where I am constantly learning, taking it all in, I think I can do something with my life.

Matt also attained a sophisticated level of global understanding from his sojourn in Tunisia, partly because he had the advantage of previous experience abroad. His family had lived in Germany when he was in high school, and he had stayed in Germany and worked after his parents returned to the States.

KNOWLEDGE ACQUISITION

Many of the students we interviewed reported that they gained specific knowledge about their host cultures. Whether they felt negative or positive toward the culture after their sojourn, students often reported that they now understood the culture better. Krista learned something about friendship patterns in Austria, Matt learned about life in the medina in Tunis, LeeAnn learned about Sri Lankan family life. Miriam, who spent a semester in France, described what she learned about French values.

> The French are very private people. But once you get to know them, you are ... a special person to them and they let you into their group and they will do absolutely anything for you.... On the other hand, the culture is more Latin than North American. It is very person-centered and families are very important. The students tend to go to universities close to home and almost all go home on the weekends. Families are more important than financial gain. The worker will take the job closer to home rather than taking a better job further away....

Denise described what she learned about cultural values in China.

> I developed some Chinese friendships ... and these served as a major bridge to the culture. I began to spend more time with these friends and less time with the student group. I met a man downtown, and my cousin and I would go visit him and his family on Sundays. They would demand your whole day. Learning that in China you cannot always say what you feel or do what you want was important. If they want you to stay a longer period of time than you had planned, you stay. In talking with them, I learned so much. They told you how they lived through the Cultural Revolution, and it amazed me what the Chinese had to go through.

Few studies have attempted to objectively assess students' increases in factual knowledge about international issues as a result of study abroad.[10] However, several studies have assessed students' self-reported increases in knowledge about the host country and/or international awareness.[11] For instance, A. O. Pfnister (1972) conducted an in-depth study of Goshen College students participating in the fourteen-week program of study and work abroad. He surveyed all 120 students in programs in Nicaragua, Costa Rica, Jamaica, Guadeloupe, West Germany, and South Korea during one trimester in 1971. He interviewed students before, during, and after the sojourn abroad and compared these interviews with those of students who had remained on the Goshen campus. He concluded that the greatest change for the study abroad group was an "awareness of different philosophies, cultures and ways of life."

In a study of students from the University of California who had been with a program in Germany, researchers found that six years later 49 percent of the students reported that an important outcome was the achievement of greater understanding of the intellectual and cultural life and traditions of the host country (Billigmeier and Forman 1975, 217–30).

Several students we interviewed also talked about their increased awareness, particularly those who encountered different political systems, like this student who lived in what was then East Germany:

> I view the world differently now because I am aware of that whole socialist system over there and the kind of limitations those people had in living out their life. In short, to learn about the different aspects of their system, the pluses and minuses, changed my worldview very much. Before I went, I really didn't know what was involved in a socialist state. So, just becoming aware of what goes on in

that part of the world and what people face there has changed my view of the world considerably.

AFFECTIVE CHANGE

Research measuring affective change is at the heart of the problem of pinning down global understanding. Unfortunately, the results obtained from the diverse methodologies used have been inconclusive and, indeed, contradictory. They are discussed in some detail in chapter 4. Suffice it to say here that the evidence which can be sifted from the research relative to affective change in the direction of global understanding indicates that the change occurs in three general categories:

1. Increased interest in international affairs/events
2. Increased world-mindedness
3. Increased cross-cultural empathy

Increased Interest in International Affairs/Events. In a number of studies, students were asked to indicate whether their interest in global issues increased because of their study abroad. In most cases, students reported such an increase as an important consequence of their experience.

Koester's studies in 1985 and 1987 revealed a significant gain in "interest in international events" for students who had been abroad for six to twelve months (vs. less than one month), for those who did voluntary or paid work, and for those who directly enrolled in foreign institutions.[12]

The students we interviewed reported that the same thing had happened to them. Krista said that she now reads the national news first, then turns directly to the international news. Matt reported that since returning from abroad, he reads everything about Tunisia, whereas before he was just curious. Mim, who lived in France, also reported a dramatic change.

> I had never been very interested in politics. But now, especially with access to a lot of publications, I follow it much more closely. I wonder if the leaders of our country realize how important the differences in culture are. After spending an entire year in France, I was more in tune with how the French think and why we think differently. There are some things that just can't be agreed upon.

The findings in this kind of self-report research are fairly consistent, showing an identifiable expansion in interest in international affairs as a result of study abroad (Pfnister 1972). However, some students feel that this interest is not reinforced when they return, partly due to the apathy on the part of their peers. For example, LeeAnn said that when she first returned from Sri Lanka, she wanted to major in something international and hoped to leave the U.S. again as soon as possible. When she realized she was staying here, it was "hard to keep feeling the international 'itch.'" She felt like she had to suppress this interest "in order to live here and be happy. . . . " Fortunately, she discovered ways to continue her international interest.

> The reentry course really helped and so did getting involved in the M.A.S.T. [Minnesota Agricultural Student Trainee] Program because it involved contact with international students, and it kept me from feeling really isolated. I felt different . . . but here in the reentry course I was surrounded by students who were *also* feeling different. So it's a good idea to help returning students get involved with international activities and international students.

Increased World-Mindedness. Perhaps the best-known objective, standardized measure of affective change in global awareness was developed by Sampson and Smith in 1957.[13] They distinguished between international-mindedness ("an interest in or knowledge about international affairs"), and world-mindedness ("a value orientation, or frame of reference, apart from knowledge about, or interest in, international relations"). A world-minded person is one who favors a global view of the problems of humanity, whose primary reference group is humanity rather than a particular nationality group, and who may or may not have a great deal of interest in and knowledge about international affairs. Likewise, a person could be internationally-minded without being world-minded.

Empirical studies using this measure have shown little change among the students in the direction of world-mindedness, but most studies so far have focused on students who have spent only a summer abroad (H.P. Smith 1955, 1957; Kafka 1968). Comments by returned students who have spent more time overseas, however, suggest that the study abroad experience does increase world-mindedness. One speaks, for example, of the "interdependency" of peoples and nations.

> I see a lot more interdependency in the world. Before I went, I had the Mexican experience, but I was pretty young, it wasn't a very strong experience. I saw all these "poor peasants in Mexico" and it wasn't clicking. Now I really see the interdependency and have a lot more respect for other cultures. I see that humanity really does have something universal that links us together, and I'm at the point where I'm a bit frustrated when I have interactions with people who don't have that same opinion, so I'm still in the growing stage. But I'm coming out of that, and I see that it is a process. There is such a multitude of perceptions and opinions in the

> world that it's unrealistic to expect that there is some kind of multicultural being that *everyone* can carry with them.

One aspect of world-mindedness is a concern for problems confronting other nations and all humankind, and an interest in finding solutions, particularly to those problems that confront developing countries and have an impact on us all (hunger, disease, etc.). To achieve this aspect of world-mindedness, most students need to be confronted with the realities of life in Third-World countries.

Several of the students we interviewed voiced this concern. Mark, who studied in Costa Rica, said,

> I was so much more aware of what was going on in the world down there than I ever was before in my life. I had heard about Nicaragua and the conflicts in the region, but I never really became interested or very aware of what was going on there. I was changed in that regard rather significantly. These were real people to me. They became my friends and I cared very much what happened to them, and I continue to care.

Research on the impact of world-mindedness has produced mixed results. One study, which asked students to recall their attitudes prior to and just after going abroad, reported significant changes. The second study, however, which actually measured students' attitudes before and after their sojourns, found that very little change occurred.[14]

Implicit in world-mindedness is the understanding that the values of one's own society are not universal and that values of other societies are just as valid. An understanding of cultural relativity is one of the most important aspects of world-mindedness. A first step in gaining this understanding may be a rather indiscriminate adoption of the values of the host culture and a rejection of one's home cultural values. However, if the student continues in the culture learning process, he or she will eventually reach a more sophisticated understanding, an "ethnorelative" perspective, or "reflective commitment"—an understanding that all cultural values may be relative—but one has to be comfortable with one's own cultural and individual values (Bennett 1986b; Perry 1970).[15]

LeeAnn described her reactions to being confronted with new religious values and her effort to reconcile these new values with the values she was taught as a child.

> My religious values were hit the hardest. They really took a beating. I spent so much time with Buddhists. I had never questioned my religion before. The Lutheran religion was really an important part of my life, but I think a lot of it was the social life it provided. I had never questioned anything. But after learning something about other religions, and seeing things—they kept questioning everything I believed in—all of a sudden *I* started questioning. They would say, "You just need your God because you're afraid to be alone." And then I'd think, "All these people can't be wrong, there has to be *something* to this."

Increased Cross-Cultural Empathy. Another important affective component of global understanding is the ability to see the world from the perspective of another culture, to understand how someone from another culture feels—from his or her point of view. Beth had been to Israel before with a group of high school students for a brief time, but it was only after a year in an Israeli university that she was able to understand, from an Israeli perspective, what she had interpreted earlier as pushy and aggressive behavior. As she explained it,

> You feel like you are surrounded by Arab countries that hate you and a world that's against you and you can't help but feel pushy and direct. You can't survive any other way. I got to understand how they think. Their whole mentality is different.... People go into the army right after high school, and even though they dread going in for three years and they complain, they would never think about leaving the country. It's just what you do. Even something that's horrible, that's what you do.

Matt had a similar kind of empathic experience.

> I have a better understanding of foreign students and, I guess, a better understanding of the Arab side of the political conflict. Before I left, I had a hard time understanding some of the extreme reactions that Arabs have concerning Israel and colonialism, and now that I've been there and I've seen it from that point of view, I can understand their reaction. I can't always know exactly what the Arab response is going to be, but it seems to me to be important for them to prove their point, and *then* go into realistic consideration of things. There's a tradition of rhetoric, of being very persuasive in your speech, and being able to speak forcefully and prove your point. They don't work on the Western model where you present your facts first and then draw your conclusions.
>
> Also, it's the way that some Arabic phrases translate into English. *Jihad,* for instance, which is translated into English as "holy war," has many meanings in Arabic depending on how you use it. It doesn't always mean war against the infidel. It

> can also mean war against your own self, "your own personal striving to get rid of evil tendencies."

These insights reflect an understanding that goes beyond factual knowledge. They relate a truly affective change in global understanding—interest, concern, and caring about the world beyond one's national or cultural boundaries.

BEHAVIORAL CHANGE

Studies of behavioral changes have used as their measure subsequent travel abroad, involvement in international activities, membership in international organizations, and internationally oriented behavior like sending gifts to or in other ways maintaining contact with overseas friends.[16]

Sue is typical of the many students who talked about future travel plans in our interviews.

> That's why I really want to do something international again, like joining the Peace Corps and living abroad. That is the big thing, and knowing that I can do it, and knowing that I won't be very happy if I stay here for a long time. I always talk in terms of *when* I go here, or *when* I go there, not *if* I ever get a two-week vacation and go somewhere again.

Bob echoed this sentiment when he said, "Finding out how neat it is to travel makes me want to travel everywhere."

Almost every student we interviewed mentioned being more involved in international affairs by joining clubs, participating in extracurricular activities, seeking out international students, and in general, finding ways to demonstrate behaviorally their newfound international perspective. Several students sought out others who had also been abroad and could share common experiences. Reentry courses helped. Gayle said, "I have this dire need to go out and meet Americans that have had this experience." She also felt a need to reach out and "internationalize" students who hadn't been abroad.

Her solution was to work with students who were preparing to go abroad by helping to administer a student exchange program. Sue got involved in a predeparture orientation, helping students who were preparing to study abroad on the same program in which she had participated. Matt worked for the student travel office on campus as a peer advisor, talking with students interested in international study and travel. Others, like Krista, volunteered to tutor international students or simply joined in international student activities.

Beth said she likes to meet Israeli students and talk to them in Hebrew or English and ask them what they think about what's going on in Israel. Another student, Clayton, who had been in Kenya, became an intern at the community international center that hosts foreign visitors and sponsors programs for international students' spouses and families.

Like Beth, many students found ways to keep using their language skills. Bob said, "I'm studying more French. I want to keep speaking French. I want to learn every other language on the face of the earth. Finding out I had a capacity to learn a language made me want to learn other things."

While most students mentioned some involvement in international activities after their return, they also noted that it was not necessarily easy to maintain this international perspective and be integrated back into their home campuses. Several students reported feeling "punished" for their international experience. For example, Matt indicated that his institution actually constructed obstacles for students who studied abroad—creating problems with financial aid, credit transfer, and registration.

Many of the changes described in this chapter are only recognized after students have returned home and had an opportunity to analyze, reflect on, and talk about their intercultural experience.

In summary, although previous research has not consistently conceptualized what is meant by the development of an international perspective, we have suggested that it encompasses changes in perceptions of home and host cultures as well as changes in knowledge, affective responses, and behavior. Results of qualitative research, as well as our experience and our interviews with students, indicate that students do, under certain conditions, develop an international perspective as a result of study abroad.

NOTES

1. These students' attitudes toward the educational system of the host culture conflict with findings of a recent study where U.S. students reported that their opinions of the educational system in their host culture were *more negative* after their experience abroad. See Carlson et al. (1990).

2. Hawes and Kealey (1981, 239–58) and Weissman and Furnham (1987, 313–26) discuss the importance of realistic expectations about an intercultural experience in calculating the subsequent impact of that experience, particularly in determining how well one adjusts and the degree of satisfaction with the overseas experience.

3. For research data on the impact of duration of stay, see Koester (1985; 1987).

4. In one of the earliest studies, H. P. Smith (1955) investigated attitude change in seven groups of high school and college students. Four experimental groups spent a summer in Europe as tourists or volunteer workers, and three control groups stayed at home. Results revealed no significant change in attitudes for any of the groups, and

Smith concluded that "a relatively brief experience in another culture has a limited impact on general attitudes" (473).

In a similar study, Kafka (1968) studied the effects of an overseas summer experience on eighty-one college students (compared to a control group). Results were not significant, which Kafka attributed to the short duration of the intercultural sojourn (a summer).

5. While Koester (1985; 1987) does not explicitly examine changes in perception of host country as an outcome, she does identify length of time as an important variable in influencing a number of other outcomes, e.g., changes in understanding host culture.

6. The program described in Sikkema and Niyekawa (1987) lasted twelve to fourteen months and included (1) a prefield-program seminar during the spring term, (2) a two-month (or more) summer field experience in another culture, and (3) a postfield-program seminar on campus during the fall term. The focus of the prefield-program seminar was on cross-cultural learning and the psychology of intercultural communication. In the field the students were given broadly defined assignments which called for them to immerse themselves in the culture in an effort to decipher the perceptual system and culture-based patterns of thinking and behaving. A field seminar was conducted and all students were required to keep journals. In the postfield-program seminar they examined and discussed their experiences and wrote summaries analyzing them from the cognitive perspectives learned in the prefield-program seminar. The quotations from the students' diaries excerpted in the book are as insightful as the writings and interview excerpts of students who have been abroad a much longer time.

7. For studies identifying degree of contact as an important variable in the study abroad experience see Hoffman and Zak, (1969, 165–71), Klineburg and Hull (1979, 50–66), and Marion (1980, 58–64).

8. Marion (1980), using location as a variable, found that those students studying in Germany acquired a more favorable perception of the host country than their peers in Italy and France did. H. P. Smith (1955, 469–77) also reported a significant decrease in favorable attitudes among those who lived or traveled in France and West Germany but an increase among those who lived or traveled in England. See also Herman 1970 (reported in Sell 1983, 138–39) and Nash (1976, 191–203). Students in the Nash study reported having unfavorable attitudes toward France. Salter and Teger (1975, 213–22) found that travel and work groups in Austria became more positive toward their host country, while those in France and Italy became less positive. Kafka (1968) found that students developed unfavorable attitudes toward their host countries of Switzerland, Spain, and the USSR.

9. In Klineburg and Hull's investigation of the international student experience in many countries, the data presented for the French sample indicated that only 13 percent of the foreign students in France reported that when they were in the company of others, those others were mainly French students.

> This was the lowest percentage among all of the eleven countries participating in this international investigation. The picture that continues to emerge is one of absence of contact between the foreign students and native people; it emerges regularly in France.... In almost every case relating to contact between foreign student respondents and natives, France and Canada regularly rank among the countries with the least frequent or regular contact.

10. T. S. Barrows (1981) developed an instrument to measure college students' global understanding. The instrument comprised three components: knowledge, affect, and language ability. The knowledge component was measured by 101 questions asking for specific factual information on the following topics: economic development, international relations, ethnicity and religion, and environment and national resources. However, in this study the instrument was used to measure student attitudes in general, not to measure the impact of study abroad or increased knowledge of the host culture.

11. For example, in Koester's study (1987) students reported that they were "more politically aware" as a result of the international experience. Specifically, those who had been abroad for six to twelve months reported more change in this area than those who had been abroad for less than one month; and those who did volunteer work and directly enrolled in a university reported more change than those who were with other Americans in the study abroad program or who traveled for recreation.

    Likewise, Hansel (1986) in a study investigating impacts of homestays abroad, found that students reportedly increased in "international awareness" as a result of their study abroad.

12. Several studies have reported modest to significant gain in interest in international affairs. See Garraty and Adams (1959), Price and Hensley (1978), Nash (1976), and Carlson et al. (1990).

13. Sampson and Smith (1957, 99–106) developed a scale to measure world-mindedness attitudes. Their scale contained thirty-two items, measuring attitudes in eight areas of international concern: religion, immigration, government, economics, patriotism, race, education, and war. The affect component in Barrows (1981) measured many of these same areas, primarily political (perceptions of eight world

issues, chauvinism, world government, etc.), on a self-report scale measuring concern ("I make an effort to meet people from other cultures").

14. Carlson and Widaman (1988) modified Barrows's instrument and measured general attitudes reflecting heightened sensibility to international issues, people, and culture. They measured change in two student groups: (1) students who had spent their junior year abroad and (2) a comparison group randomly selected from the same institution who stayed on campus. Students were asked to remember retrospectively their attitudes prior to and just after the year in question. Statistical analyses revealed that the study abroad group showed higher levels in all three areas measured: cross-cultural interest, cultural cosmopolitanism, and international political concern. These factors are all similar to Barrows's affective measure in that they measure interest, concern, and feeling toward global issues. In a later study (Carlson et al. 1990) they used the same items as a pre- and postmeasure for study abroad groups. Results revealed that the study abroad group was higher than the comparison group on two factors: peace and cooperation, and cultural interest and respect—both before and after study abroad—but there was no difference in the international concern factor. And neither group increased significantly between administrations of the pre-and postmeasures.

15. The ideas dealt with in these writings are discussed more extensively in the following chapter.

16. H.P. Smith (1955) and Abrams (1979, 176–87) reported that study abroad students increased their involvement in international activities after studying abroad. Carlson et al. (1990) identified a factor, international activities, that included two items: actual participation in activities aimed at effecting greater international understanding and memberships in organizations concerned with international issues and problems. However, this was a weak factor and was not used in subsequent analyses of differences between study abroad and control groups.

CHAPTER FOUR

PERSONAL DEVELOPMENT ABROAD

This chapter describes the potential impact of study abroad on students' personal development in the following areas:

1. *Intrapersonal understanding*
2. *Interpersonal relationships*
3. *Values*
4. *Life direction/vocation*

The study abroad research suggests that students who can be described as less developmentally mature before they begin their study abroad are more likely to experience a greater magnitude of personal change than those who are more mature.

Students who begin at a higher level of maturity are more likely to reach a sophisticated level of international understanding. Also, the less developmentally mature person who has only superficial contact with the host culture exhibits little change in either personal development or international awareness.

Difficulty in reentry into the home culture appears to be related to the magnitude of personal change and the attitudes of the sojourners and their families and friends. The greater the change, the more likely it is that the reentry will be difficult. However, friends and family can make a positive contribution by trying to understand the ways in which the student has changed and help the student incorporate those changes into the life back home.

When students grow intellectually and gain a new understanding of the world, they discover that they are changed people. They begin to relate differently to others and to think about themselves and their futures in new ways. In this chapter we will examine how study abroad affects this inner landscape.

We know that individuals develop in different ways and at a different pace. For some students, the time abroad leads to personal changes that are rapid and far-reaching. For others, the experience is not so transforming.[1] Why the difference? Research suggests that those students who can be described as less developmentally mature prior to the study abroad experience but who dive into the local culture and open themselves thoroughly to contact with the local culture are the ones who demonstrate the most personal growth. Students who are more mature at the start report greater change in their understanding of the other culture and in their appreciation for its values. Those students who report little change in global awareness and personal maturation are those who can be described as less mature developmentally and who—for whatever reason—have only superficial contact with the culture.[2] Our interviews with students who went abroad support these findings.

Don, who went on the Goshen SST program to Costa Rica, is an example of a student who matured a great deal because of his experience abroad. Before going, he could have been described as an insecure person, uncertain about his life direction, counterdependent in his relationships with peers and authority figures, dualistic in his way of thinking, and fairly ethnocentric. His view of success was "to make as much money as possible." With great hesitation he agreed to participate in the program. In chapter 1 we learned how profoundly the experience affected him.

Because the host families in Costa Rica accepted Don for who he was, he grew in self-confidence and social grace. He developed a new sense of security, based on his ability to adapt to new situations rather than on his money-earning potential. He learned that he could "live happily without great material resources." Don did not narrow his career options during his months abroad; other maturing processes had to come first. But he did return with new priorities.

> I don't expect to be paid for everything I do, to get rich no matter what it takes.... Whatever I do I am going to do to the best of my ability and if I am

> successful monetarily, good, and if not, I have given it my best shot.

Meanwhile, as we have noted, his motivation to study increased considerably, and after he returned, he received the best grades of his college career.

Mike was another Goshen student who lacked a great deal of self-confidence before entering the SST program. Though he was at a different place developmentally from Don, he had also expended a great deal of energy during his first two years at Goshen grappling with issues of identity and life direction. These issues were far from resolved at the time he departed for Jena, in what was then East Germany.

> The biggest change that I made as a result of my Study Service Term was that I grew up. I gained vision inside and outside of myself. I have the ability to progress. I won't have to be stuck in one place the rest of my life.

Don and Mike both believed that if they could have another experience abroad, they would gain even more from it. They now felt more ready to immerse themselves in a new culture. Mike called his time in Germany "kind of a warm-up" and said that the next time he would be able to absorb more of the world around him. "Now that I have gained this understanding, I would make more contacts and I would push myself harder. I have moved beyond survival and would be ready to move into a deeper involvement in the culture."

Don and Mike also reported increased global awareness. However, in this area they were surpassed by Clayton and Margarita, who were more personally secure and whose level of confidence freed them to get involved with their host cultures. Margarita, the Goshen art student who went to China, was described by her peers and professors as a very self-assured person who had solid friendships and an open mind. She said, "My previous experience abroad in Haiti helped me gain the personal insight I needed to greatly assist my entry into the Chinese culture." Clayton, who participated in the Minnesota Studies in International Development program in Kenya, was fairly independent, secure, confident, and relativistic in his thinking before his departure for study abroad. Clayton did not report great leaps in personal maturation as a result of his study abroad. He spoke instead of a considerable increase in global understanding and international concerns. This change was apparently possible because of his level of maturity before departure. He put it succinctly: "I immersed myself without dissolving, and I identified without adopting."

Margarita's friendship with a Chinese artist became a significant cultural bridge for her. "Art was the medium which facilitated my immersion into the Chinese culture." After about two months, she began to leave behind her Western approach and to understand the Chinese concept of art. Once she had made this advance in understanding the culture, she became more involved with her Chinese fellow students. Until then she had kept her distance. For Margarita the four-month term was too short.

> Only after four months did I start to understand, because it takes a while to get rid of preconceived ideas. Once I was willing to accept other perspectives, I could understand a great deal more of the total culture.

Lori is an example of a student whose term abroad was not a time of personal growth. Her frame of reference for seeing the world had been pretty much the same for several years before she went abroad. And she said that adjustment wasn't easy for her. She reported little change in her personal development or in her global understanding. She did not become involved with her host family (partly due to the lack of language ability and not wanting to feel stupid) or with other nationals and, hence, was unable to see the world from any other perspective than the one with which she grew up.

> I felt a lot of negative things when I was there. I felt guilty about that because I had heard that SST was supposed to be the most wonderful thing in the world. I was disappointed that it was so much harder than I thought it would be. Some situations I can adjust to rather easily, but when they are off the wall, I just go wacko. That SST experience was pretty much off the wall. I was very glad to get back and be somewhere where I could be understood and I didn't have to worry about that all of the time.

The reasons for the differences in these students' levels of personal growth are not as clear as they may seem. A review of the research on personal development abroad reveals several problems. Most are similar to those we mentioned for research on the international perspective. First, the term itself is not used in a uniform manner. In some studies personal development refers to a range of dimensions from autonomy to world-mindedness while in others it refers more narrowly to dimensions associated with social skills, autonomy, self-confidence, self-esteem, self-reliance, or self-concept.

Another problem is a contradiction in the findings of various kinds of studies. As with research on the international perspective, three categories of instruments have been used in assessing change: (1) standardized instruments, (2) specifically designed instruments, and (3) self-report or interview-type questionnaires. Once again, data from the self-report approach indicated more impact from the study abroad experience than did the specially designed instruments, and these revealed more impact than the standardized measures. While standardized studies often reflect little relationship between personal change and studying abroad, questionnaires and interviews with students almost always associate positive personal growth with the experience of studying abroad.[3]

Why such a difference? Do studies using standardized instruments reflect the absence of true change or are they simply an inadequate means of measuring this sort of change? Do those studies using instruments specifically developed for study abroad—such as interviews and questionnaires—identify aspects of personal change that standardized tests have been unable to measure? Few of the studies paid attention to variables that complicate the relationship between intercultural contact and personal change—beginning level of maturity, depth of contact, length of stay, or location.

To discern change, a study should track the progress of the same individuals over time (Barber 1983, 7–10). But this kind of study—the matched longitudinal design—has some inherent shortcomings. Attitude scales can be unreliable because of the respondents' moods or states of mind, and scoring is fraught with difficulties (Bereiter 1963; Feldman and Newcomb 1969; Treanor 1970; Feldman 1972).

Debra Sell (1981, 16), a Kent State University researcher, observed that all these studies "have lacked a theoretical base upon which further research can be assessed." In spite of this, Anne Ellison and Bennett Simon (1973), after reviewing the literature, suggested that the difficulties in measuring change (related to the diverse nature of individual change and the prevalence of methodological and statistical problems) should not be cause for devaluing change studies entirely. Instead, they saw these problems as good reason to supplement and validate such studies with other methods: interviews, participant observation in the anthropological style, home visits, and questionnaires designed to elicit information about the change process.

Winter, McClelland, and Stewart (1981), who studied the effects of a liberal arts education on students, argue that

> concern for quick and easy measurement often has usurped a concern for meaningful content of what is measured.... In the personality or affective domain of college effects, many researchers have used standardized inventories or scales, seemingly because they exist rather than because the constituent variables or scales are particularly relevant to the manifest or latent goals of liberal education. Therefore, even if the change score accurately reflects the respondent's change, the change may not be relevant to the stated purposes and goals of a given program or to the purposes of the institution (22).[4]

The same applies to scores that reflect a *lack* of change.

In this chapter, personal development connotes a process of unfolding, growth, evolution, expansion, and maturation of the individual self. Our approach will not be to mimic the central task of developmental psychology—to study the developmental process itself. Rather, our purpose here is to describe the impact of study abroad on four aspects of personal development: (1) intrapersonal, (2) interpersonal, (3) values, and (4) life direction/vocation. These components of development were selected not because of a particular developmental framework but because they best reflected the categories of personal development used in study abroad literature.

In the following pages intrapersonal development refers to changes in various characteristics of the inner self, such as self-esteem, autonomy, self-confidence, self-reliance, and self-differentiation. Interpersonal development relates to social skills and to the quality of interaction with other individuals and groups of individuals. Values include ultimate beliefs which guide the making of decisions, the central principles that give direction and meaning to each individual's life. Finally, life direction/vocation is described as the unique expression of the self in the environment, the use of one's abilities and talents to do what needs doing in the world.

INTRAPERSONAL DEVELOPMENT

The majority of the studies which have focused on change in intrapersonal development through study abroad have identified variables related to intrapersonal functioning: a positive change in self-concept, an enhanced self-confidence and self-esteem, a higher level of self-reliance, and an increase in independence or autonomy.[5] The contrast in results, however, is pronounced. Only a few of the studies that used standardized measures found study abroad to have a significant impact; a number found no significant change.[6] However, the majority of studies which utilized self-report questionnaires and interviews did reveal changes in the intrapersonal dimensions.[7]

One of the problems with the self-report approach is the lack of uniformity and basis for comparison between studies. For instance, the meaning given to *self-reliance* by one researcher is the same as that given to the term *independence* or even *autonomy* by a second or third researcher.[8] Likewise, *self-esteem* in some studies means the same as *self-confidence* in others.[9] And still other studies utilizing self-report data do not use the term *self-confidence* at all (Pfnister 1979; Koester 1985).

In her study of the U.S. student abroad, Koester (1984) summarizes the difficulties of interpreting the research.

> Interpreting research studies which investigate the impact of intercultural contact for U.S. students is

> difficult for several reasons. The differing conclusions researchers have come to stem from the variety of variables which have been investigated. Furthermore, even those variables which have remained fairly constant from one study to the next have been operationalized differently. Assumptions which originally suggested a simplistic relationship between contact and effect have been challenged, but not systematically explored and exposed.
>
> Students, for example, in different types of international contact situations (work vs. travel vs. study) are compared to each other when the dynamics of the particular situations may be so different as to render a comparison nonsensical (4).

Here we will focus on three principal dimensions of intrapersonal development: (1) self-awareness, (2) self-confidence, and (3) autonomy (self-reliance/independence).

Self-Awareness. Self-awareness and cultural awareness are inseparable (Adler 1975; Hall 1977). In his book, *Pastoral Counseling across Cultures,* David Augsburger (1986) discusses a theology of presence.

> Presence requires an integration of self-awareness with an awareness of the other.... In knowing the other, one comes to know the self more deeply; in knowing oneself, one is opened to perceive and receive the other more fully (37).

Understanding and transcending culture cannot be accomplished without some degree of self-awareness. Living abroad provides potent new experiences that give ample opportunity to see oneself in a new light. Even though few studies have documented change in this area, we suspect that changes in awareness are inevitable for students who have quality contact with another culture.

Sue, of the University of Minnesota, became more aware that she liked to "problem solve ... to be in the dark about things and to be on the edge of discovering something." She also discovered that being shy and not speaking up right away makes you a "better observer, more respectful of other people's cultures or values.... I didn't know that about myself before I went abroad."

For Barb from Goshen College, having a reference group during the first part of her sojourn in Jena, Germany, was not only a crucial bridge into the culture but a powerful tool in the expansion of her self-understanding. After the group members got to know each other pretty well, she began to "experience real acceptance."

> When you experience this acceptance, you accept yourself at that level and then you are free to go beyond where you had been before.... I got in touch with some things about myself as a result of the small-group dynamics (there was some real confronting that went on). I learned what other people thought of me, and as a result my view of myself became more congruent with how others perceived me. I would share how I saw myself, and others would tell me how they saw me. That really is a very helpful process when people are observing you in that kind of a situation for so long.

This freeing up of herself moved her into the culture.

> ... to take off on a train to another city and find relatives there and to explore things, to research things, and to meet strange people and talk German for hours ... being able to experience my German

> language facility developing was really an incredible feeling.

Self-Confidence. To have self-confidence and a positive view of oneself is to be aware, honest, and secure in oneself and in relationships with others (Hansel 1986). A large number of students interviewed associated their study abroad experience with an increase in their self-confidence, or self-esteem.

Bob, from the University of Minnesota, said that being abroad "helped my confidence . . . the best thing was finding out that people liked me." Because his French was weak at first, he had to project a core self "without having the verbal capacity," which he had thought was crucial to acceptance from others. His self-confidence increased in ways he had not previously experienced.

Don said he became "a much more outgoing, more social, and more self-confident person." Of these three changes, which he said were "tied together," the increase in self-confidence was the most important to him.

Denise, a Goshen College student who studied and worked in China, grew in confidence through a new understanding of herself and by discovering she was up to the challenge.

> I now realize that I am flexible and confident enough that I could survive in extreme situations. I can live without luxuries, and I can live in a culture that is different from my own. This is a real confidence builder. I may have thought I could do all this before SST, but this experience tested it for me and makes it more certain.

Research carried out by Bandura (1986) indicates that self-confidence increases when a person successfully meets a number of challenges. Randy, another of the Goshen students who went to Jena, Germany, said that he made gains in his self-confidence when he found he could get along in German.

> It helped me a lot to know that I could communicate.... I am basically pretty shy in asking people for help. Out on the street I had to. I would have been lost otherwise. The added difficulty of needing to use the German language to meet basic needs makes you realize how much easier it is to cope in your own culture, using your own language. You're confident that you can do anything.

Autonomy (Self-Reliance/Independence). Individuals who feel they have little say in the decisions that affect them probably will not have a high degree of self-confidence or self-esteem. In fact, individuals who have little control over their lives will likely experience at least some level of depression. Sharon Parks (1986), who has studied and written extensively about young adult development, has written that the "form of dependence" (dependent, inner-dependent, interdependent) is a manifestation of relationship: "Dependence is an inevitable dimension of the power of the relation of self and other.... Humans are always and necessarily interdependent beings, but the form, experience, and awareness of dependence changes" (77). During the maturation process a person whose sense of the world "is dependent upon an uncritically assumed Authority" develops, after several in-between stages, to the point where the "locus of primary trust now resides neither in the assumed authority of another nor in the courageously claimed authority of the inner self. Rather, trust is now centered in the meeting of self and other ... [that is, in] interdependence."

Many students leave for study abroad as dependent individuals. The experience abroad provides the kind of challenge that assists the student in becoming more independent and self-reliant. Self-report data is full of testimony from students attributing increases in their self-reliance and independence to their sojourn abroad.

Deb, a Goshen sophomore who studied and worked in Costa Rica, is a dramatic example of this type of change.

> When I was on service, I was basically by myself.... There were a lot of decisions that I had to make on my own, and I couldn't go to my parents or a friend. It was so hard to translate and talk to someone in Spanish that I just decided that I had to make this or that decision on my own. There was nowhere else to turn! I had to go on my own instinct and judgment, and that was a pretty big switch for me. The language barrier made me realize that I am really on my own because not many people know how I feel. I can't depend on them very well....
>
> When I arrived on service I was very scared and felt very helpless. I thought to myself, "Oh, I can't believe that I am going to be here for six weeks! How am I going to make it through without knowing the language that well and no one around that I can go talk to?" But there was no one I could run to and say, "Help me." So I was pushed to be on my own and make it. That is what I ended up doing.

Krista was another who said that the biggest personal change resulting from her semester in Austria was that she became more independent. "I rely on myself rather than other people, and that has to do with my experience."

Beth, who spent eleven months studying in a university in Israel, reflected on her move toward independence and self-reliance in relationship to her mother and the use of money.

> All my life I've had my Mom to fall back on. I could call her and say "Mom, how can I do this? Can you do my laundry?" But all of last year, it was like, "Oh my God, the banks are closed, I'm not going to eat until Sunday!" It changes your attitude. You become more aware of what's going on around you. You can't just let things go sliding by and assume that someone is going to come and take care of you.
>
> I also learned more about money. I went through more money in the first few weeks, and all of a sudden I realized I might go through $10,000 in the year.

For Mike, the development of self-reliance came the last couple of weeks of his stay in Germany.

> I spent two weeks traveling after the fourteen-week experience in Germany, and I found I was able to get around if I wanted to. I had enough knowledge, street smarts, enough intelligence in general that I was able to communicate and allow myself to survive. Self-reliance increased a great deal. I came to the realization that if I can make it in a foreign culture, I can make it in my own culture.

INTERPERSONAL DEVELOPMENT

Not only does personal development mean differentiation of one's self from others, but it also means integration of the self with others. Study abroad provides a fertile environment for the furtherance of this kind of integration, what we are calling interpersonal development. It introduces students to different cultures, providing the opportunity for them to open their minds to people with different ideas and values, and maybe even to begin to appreciate the differences in such a way that their lives will be enriched and their network of belonging expanded. In a more subtle way the study abroad experience releases the students from their present peer group and frees them to recompose their criteria for their friendships. It can free them to ask new questions, try new interests, and form new conceptions of life.

A number of studies (James 1976; Pace 1959; Stauffer 1973; Pfnister 1972 and 1979) have associated an increase in interpersonal skills with study abroad, either in a general way or in increased tolerance of people who are different.

During interviews a number of students indicated that their experience abroad had an impact on their interpersonal development. Some opened themselves to a broader range of people, some changed friendship groups upon return, and others improved their communication skills, which enhanced their relationships with existing friends and helped them to make new ones.

LeeAnn said that her experience in Sri Lanka gave her new insight into her connectedness—or lack of it—with her family.

> I have really suppressed my changed attitudes toward family. I don't think they fit in back in this culture. I don't think we [my family] communicate at all. We really don't talk. I don't think we know anything about each other's lives. We're supposedly a perfect American family, and I don't think we communicate at all. And I try—at Christmas I suggested that we try to self-disclose a little, and that didn't go over well at all. The response was, "We know these things about each other." So I've learned to accept my family for what they are, and I'm not going to change them, and that's OK.

> With my friends, I don't like to party as much, don't have to be where the action is; just being with one friend is OK. Being with friends who are very fashion-conscious, I feel inadequate, but when I leave them, I'm fine.

Barb's study abroad group in Germany, which fostered the expansion of her self-concept, was not made up of any of her friends from back on campus. The students who made up this group did not hold her to old values, and she felt secure enough to reach out into the culture and become more than she could have imagined before the experience. When students who already constitute a group at home go abroad together, the group can function as an inhibiting force in interpersonal development because of carryover of peer group pressure from home to host culture and, perhaps, because it serves as a retreat from growth-producing experiences in the new environment.

Don, a Goshen student in Costa Rica, found his study abroad group to be a helpful bridge into the culture in a similar way to Barb.

> It was good to have a group like this at the beginning. The group functioned as a support group [these were individuals that I didn't know before going] that assisted me in moving into the culture. In addition, I learned from the experience of other members of the group. They were very supportive and shared very openly and freely about what they were learning. I was more ready to branch out on my own in the service assignment the last six weeks of the trimester after this very positive start.

Not only was the study abroad group important for Don's growth in building relationships but so also was the development of friendships in the culture.

> As I said earlier, how I view people is the number one change. I now value people and value knowing what is going on in the world.
>
> I made this very good friend while I was there. He really showed me the country and interpreted the culture to me. He was the most important factor in helping me understand and enjoy Costa Rica. Who in our culture would take the time he took for me? I only knew him for three or four weeks, but in that time we became very close. By the end of my term I could talk with him about anything that was on my mind, and he could do the same with me. I mean, we had nothing to hide. Getting really close to someone like that really meant a lot beyond getting to know the culture. This friendship was of lasting value.

For Goshen student Phil, the Costa Rican host family was a vital connection and bridge into the culture. He shared his thoughts and feelings openly with them, deepening his understanding of life and his ability to relate to others.

> Evenings my family and I really had fun. Maybe my Mom would say something that I wouldn't understand, and I would get out the dictionary. She was really some person—always trying to pick up English. She even went dancing with us one night. Four of us friends were at the dance, and here she showed up with her son-in-law. She stayed with us until one or two in the morning and walked back the one or two miles home with us.

> The oldest daughter and I really had in-depth discussions, and I learned a great deal about the culture from her. She shared a lot of her frustrations of being out in the Western world for a while and having to come back and fit in again.
>
> Having a career and getting married were not compatible. If she didn't get married, she would not be understood. If she got married, she would have to give up her career, which involved a lot of travel. She was really struggling and torn.

Goshen student Kay learned new ways to relate to others on SST.

> When I was in China, I learned to totally open myself up to others. I wasn't afraid to be laughed at after I was there for a while. We were constantly asked to perform. Before that experience that kind of request would have made me very nervous. Poetry reading and singing were some of the ways in which I shared myself with them. Now I look back at how vulnerable I allowed myself to be—those were some of the best times. I *learned* to be vulnerable over there. . . . I had money stolen on a bus. I had a person raging, screaming at me. I just started crying because there was nothing else to do. Now when I look back, it makes me laugh. . . . I laughed in China, mostly at myself, more than I ever laughed in my life. Maybe it was a way to handle stress. There was never a dull moment.

DEVELOPMENT OF VALUES

In addition to intra- and interpersonal development, taking responsibility for the shaping of one's values and for the consequent decisions and behavior is an important aspect of the personal development process. Parks (1986) says that the "threshold of young adulthood is marked by the capacity to take self-aware responsibility for choosing the path of one's own fidelity" (77). Confrontation with the values of other cultures helps students to reexamine their own values, fostering a reshaping of the principles that guide behavior.

A number of studies (C.T. Smith 1971; Billigmeier and Forman 1975; Abrams 1979; Pfnister 1979; Pyle 1981) have associated study abroad with changes in values. Some studies didn't use the term *values* but referred to "liberalization of attitudes" (Leonard 1959; Marion 1974), to specific values such as "policies which promote the freer exchange of ideas, goods and people among nations" (Pace 1959), or to altruism (Kauffmann 1982).

The student interviews provided important clues about the shaping of values abroad. As with the other two areas of personal development, the quality of the contact in the host culture is apparently an important influence on the magnitude of change.

Bob found that the biggest change he experienced while studying in France was the "continuation of a process" that he had started a few years before "of deconstructing all the myths of U.S. culture" and the discovery of what would make him happy. Prior to departure he said he was very sexist but was in the process of breaking out of it. After a relationship with a French woman, which was "an intercultural disaster," he began to realize that his view of women was made up of "myths that needed to be broken." By the end of his experience he said, "I was getting to be comfortable with myself, beginning to look at things the way they really are, from a completely different point of view, and seeing how false my previous perspective was."

LeeAnn says she became a much less competitive person as a result of her experience abroad.

> I almost completely lost my competitiveness. I was very competitive in high school. In terms of my long-term goal, I wanted to work in a big corporation. Now, it's "OK, let me make my little corner of the world better."

Don's values changed nearly 180 degrees during his stay in Costa Rica. He came to feel that relationships and helping others were more important goals than driving ambition and amassed wealth. And he began to systematize his thinking.

> I still struggle with the tension between the work ethic/efficiency emphasis of the U.S. and the emphasis on relationships in Costa Rica. Relationships become lost in the work ethic of the U.S. In Costa Rica it is a total swing of the spectrum. Presently, I say shoot for the middle of the road. People are important, but there has to be a middle way.

Altruism, unselfish consideration of the welfare of others, emerged as a significant value for Goshen student Mark.

> Just being able to help people [service gave us that opportunity down there] was very fulfilling to me. For instance, I taught basketball on my service assignment, and when I saw the kid make a basket and look at me with his beaming smile, that really made me feel good. To think that I had a hand in helping someone along means a lot. Teaching someone how to shoot a basket or dribble a ball is not

> any big monumental thing, but nonetheless, I saw the fruits of being helpful in that little way. Service, therefore, was a very big aspect of the program to me. In summary I have now aligned myself with the essence of Jesus's mission—to give myself to the needs of other people.

DEVELOPMENT OF LIFE DIRECTION/VOCATION

Finding a direction in life, a vocation, is the capstone of personal development. It is what Keniston (1960) calls "questions of social role and lifestyle, or questions of relationship to the existing society" (6). Finding a fit between one's unique, emerging self and the larger society is an important and ongoing task in the Western adult world. Some authorities in the area of developmental psychology suggest that the achievement of self-awareness (made up of the other three strands of development: intrapersonal, interpersonal, and values development) and the achievement of an effective social role is a process consisting of two distinct steps, rather than something that occurs in a single continuous stream (Keniston 1960; Chickering 1969). Encounters with our world may foster development in self-awareness, but

> the task of integrating the critically aware self with integrity into society, in a way that is both effective and satisfying, may now (in this age) represent a second developmental task on the other side of the emergence of critical thought and inner dependence (Parks 1986, 80).

Studying or living abroad often forces students to think about life direction because they encounter new ways of being in the social order. Most students will not be ready to decide how they will be involved in society beyond college, but they will almost surely wrestle with the questions central to vocational choice: Who am I? Who am I going to be? Where am I? Where am I going?

If this concept of development as a two-step process is at all on target, then the educational community may have to revise the goals of study abroad related to vocational development. The assumption that a positive study abroad experience will help the student narrow vocational options is incorrect in many cases. Many young adult students returning from study abroad may have broadened their options rather than narrowed them. Given the developmental level of most students, they will likely return with a wider variety of options for their place in society than when they left.

The results of the Carlson study (Carlson et al. 1990) indicate that the study abroad students tended to be more open with regard to career choice than the comparison group, which tended to be more set in direction. A substantial number of study abroad students noted that career factors were significant to them in electing to study abroad. For example, students planning careers in international business viewed the upcoming experience abroad as almost essential to their career development. The perceived significance of the sojourn abroad for later career development is underscored by the fact that between 87 and 95 percent of the study abroad students felt that they would be able to utilize the international experience in their later professional life.

The interviews illustrate the findings of the research and underscore the complexity of finding one's place in society, especially one that is viewed more globally. Choosing a career is only one facet of this larger task.

Don, who demonstrated so much change in the other three strands of personal development, remained undecided about occupational choices. That task loomed on the horizon. For a number of upper-class students, the time abroad expanded the options of an already chosen direction. Denise discovered she had "the gift to communicate to people of other cultures." So she began to think about expanding her economics major to international economics. Mark, a junior biology major, stayed in biology but realized that helping people was central to his life's purposes. Biology was one of the tools he would use to do this. Mike was an art major who, after living in Germany, wanted to become "an artist with political awareness, an artist with a social conscience." He believes that "artists who can successfully incorporate issues into their work are able to have a very powerful message and impact on society." Another Goshen student, Kristi, said that being in Germany reinforced her career choice of elementary education because of the way the German culture valued children. She now wants her students to have the same opportunity she has had, to learn "to appreciate another kind of person different from themselves." One of her goals is to incorporate the "outcast, the handicapped, the minority students, and other marginalized people" by being sure their perspective is heard and understood.

For some students the sojourn abroad was a catalyst for finding some vocational direction or for changing that direction. Jennifer, who had no sense of direction before her experience in China, found herself moving toward the selection of a sociology major upon her return. Shana discovered that she "really enjoyed teaching English" in China and as a result came back and took a teaching English as a second language (TESL) education minor, shifted to an interdisciplinary major, and was "able to firm up some decisions" as to what she wanted to do after college as well. Kay's experience in China "definitely influenced" her choice of vocation. She discovered that she really liked teaching and, like Shana, came back and took a TESL program.

PERSONAL DEVELOPMENT AND REENTRY

Several studies (Lank 1983; Martin 1986; Uehara 1986) have explored reentry adjustment issues. In general, relationships between parents (especially mothers) and students improve over the time the students are gone, but romantic relationships and friendships suffer. The only relationships with friends that seem to improve are with those individuals who have had similar overseas experience, or with older brothers and sisters with whom the students have more in common. A couple of studies (Abrams-Reis 1980; Churchill 1958) have provided evidence that a lack of emotional support during the reentry period may have significant influence on how the experience abroad is perceived and integrated into the student's future life.[10]

The interviews illustrate these findings rather well. For some students reentry is not difficult. Most students, however, express some degree of stress in returning to the North American culture. As we noted earlier, it appears that the more immersed the student becomes in the host culture, the more difficult the reentry. Students like Lori, who had negative experiences abroad, were only superficially involved with the culture, and changed little as a result, found reentry fairly easy. Those who became immersed to any degree found that they had changed more, and as a result, reentry was more difficult. Some experienced alienation from family and close friends because they had become different people while abroad. A number of these reacted negatively to their home culture, rejecting its attitudes, values, beliefs, and behavior patterns. Acceptance of the changed self by others as well as by the sojourner seemed to be the key to a healthy reentry adjustment. Students who felt pressure to revert back to what they were before the experience had more difficulty adjusting upon return than those who were allowed to incorporate their changes into their daily living.

Don reported a very rocky reentry. He said he was constantly in a bad mood and often very irritable. In addition to the contrast in the pace of life, he was also upset by the lack of closeness in his own family in contrast to what he had experienced with his Costa Rican family. More importantly,

> My natural family wanted me to be the person I was before I left. They were not really accepting me as I was in the way I had changed. That was disconcerting. I remember people making remarks like, "What has happened to you? You have really changed a lot." Yes I had, but that negative connotation was really a thorn in my side. I wished they could have celebrated the changes with me.

Upon her return from China, Denise expressed shock at the many things she had forgotten about the United States: the many nationalities, the large sizes of so many people, and the rich variety in the color of clothes. The second shocker was going Christmas shopping with her mother very soon after her arrival home. She was so overwhelmed that she had to go wait in the car. Her family was a very important support in her adjustment, but it took longer to get back into the swing of things with her friends back on the campus.

> In my confusion I was glad I could be with my family, people who knew me, cared for me, and allowed me to adjust to things. They allowed me to be who I was as a changed person. They didn't have expectations of me on how I should act. That was helpful.
>
> When I came back to school, my friends were really open to me. However, I felt an independence

> that I had not felt as strongly as before. It did take me awhile to get back into the swing of it. The things that I thought would be difficult, like food and clothes, weren't really the problem. The things that were difficult were absolutes and dogmas based on the Western mentality and worldview. I could relate to that kind of conversation and conviction very well, but I now knew that view wasn't the only way of looking at things. The surface things like clothes, food, and watching TV weren't hard to adjust to, but the deeper issues were much more difficult.
>
> How to relate and share what I learned about myself and the world as a result of my experience in China was and is difficult. People get turned off or tired of hearing, "When I was in China, I learned that there is a different view." I soon learned to take a more roundabout approach by stating some of the things directly as my ideas rather than referring back to China. When I did this, people wondered, "Now where did she come up with that idea?" This approach opened the door to more conversation and resulted in less alienation. It demonstrated that people can be different, and it is not an absolute that people will not understand you. This approach seems more acceptable than saying in effect, "I have an experience and you can't understand because you have not been there."

Some students upon their return to campus form new patterns of affiliation; the old groups are no longer adequate. Kay and Jennifer found moving back into their peer groups difficult. Kay didn't answer phone calls from her friends for about a week after her return.

> Here I was, [I] had this huge experience and people here are just "ho hum" and not too curious as to what took place. That is frustrating because you know that so much has happened in your life, but people are more curious about whether you have interest in this guy anymore, or whatever—they don't care about what happened to you during your experience in China.

Jennifer found herself associating with different people than she had before—people she learned to know in China and other individuals who reflected the type of person she had become.

> Knowing that I had changed, knowing more concretely what I had decided about things in relationships and choosing what is important—I knew that it was going to make coming back to campus and to people here difficult. I was worried about how they would respond. That created unease in me.
>
> Upon return it was hard being around people. I sat and observed people for a while to see how they had regrouped themselves. I had become better friends with some people from SST and got to know some other new people. So I am not with the same people I was with prior to SST because I don't want to be any more. It was uncomfortable for about a month until I got used to being here again.

Barb expressed a real need to process in depth what she had experienced in Jena, Germany.

> I had so many stories. I shared some in my Pinch Penny book [campus publication], and of course we got together as a group, but somehow I just didn't

> feel I had adequate context to share my stories. It just doesn't seem to do justice to the experience. It is not that I am just nostalgic—remember Jena, remember Jena. It is deeper than that. It is not just looking back but looking forward. How can we continue those ways of learning here?

Difficulty in reentry into the home culture appears to be related to the magnitude of personal change and the attitudes of the sojourners and their family and friends. The greater the change the more likely the chance that reentry will be difficult. Students who attempted to, or felt pressure to, revert back to what they were before their departure had more difficulty adjusting upon return than those who were allowed to incorporate the changes into their lives.

NOTES

1. See synthesis (Appendix, Table 1) of findings from research about study abroad.

2. See Allport (1954); Amir (1969); Hensley and Sell (1979); Hoffman and Zak (1969); Koester (1985); Leonard (1964); Marion (1974); Pyle (1981); Hopkins (1982); Craig (1983); Bresee (1985); McGhee (1983); Salter and Teger (1975); C.T. Smith (1971).

    This literature contains discussion about the influence of two variables (preexisting attitudes of the student and the quality of contact that the student has with the host culture) on the magnitude of change. The level of maturation and its relationship to magnitude of change is one of the preexisting conditions that has been the focus of only two of these studies: Pyle and McGhee. (Hopkins and Bresee indicate it is a factor that needs to be accounted for.)

    McGhee found that there was a significant difference between students from the study abroad group who started off at different developmental positions. The students who started off with the lowest pretest scores showed the greatest change, while those who had higher scores actually showed a tendency to regress on the post-test. McGhee concluded that students studying abroad who start off at lower developmental positions appear to change more than those who begin at higher levels. He speculated that the experience of studying abroad meets the developmental needs of students at lower positions better than those starting out further along.

While the rest of the studies do not focus on maturation level as a preexisting condition, if one reads the self-report data and some of the specially designed study results, a sense of how different maturation levels influence personal change begins to take shape. Further empirical studies designed to expand on the McGhee study would be most valuable.

3. Kafka (1968) speaks to the problem of instrumentation. "While seeking appropriate instrumentation in the vague field of attitude change the researcher has to choose between standardized tests which are of proven quality but have not yet detected change from cross-cultural exposure, or locally devised tests in which the reliability and validity are questionable" (121).

4. For a more complete discussion of the problems associated with the measurement of change, see Kauffmann (1982).

5. Positive change in self-concept: Leonard (1959); Hoeh and Spuck (1975, 220–26); Carsello and Greiser (1976, 276–78).

   Increased self-confidence: James (1976, 559–607); Pfnister (1972); Pelowski (1979); Lamet and Lamet (1982); Koester (1985).

   Increased self-esteem: Hensley and Sell (1979); James (1976); Price and Hensley (1978).

   Increased self-reliance: Billigmeier and Forman (1975, 217–30); Pfnister (1972 and 1979); Kauffmann (1982).

   Increased independence/autonomy: Pyle (1981, 509–14); Billigmeier and Forman (1975); Nash (1976, 191–203).

6. Standardized studies which found some impact on intrapersonal development include Hensley and Sell (1979) and Pyle (1981). Studies which report no significant impact are Kafka (1968) and McGuigan (1958, 55–60). McGuigan concluded, "Modifications of the personality as a result of intercultural experiences are rather rare" (59).

   See also Morgan (1972). Even though Morgan found no significant change in personal development, he did discover a relationship between personality types and adaptation patterns as exemplified in the two extreme types: Type A, the cultural relativists, and Type E, culture opposites. Each adapted differently to the cross-cultural experience so that it became a different kind of learning experience for each individual. The Type A cultural relativist was better able to adapt, cope, and empathize with people than Type E, the cultural opposite. Adaptation for the cultural opposite meant closer ties with American peers, an intense nostalgia for home, and a heightened nationalism as opposed to a movement toward global loyalties.

It would be important to know what factors contribute to the makeup of the cultural opposite. For instance, how would this type of person rate on McGhee's maturity scale? If the type of contact with the host culture could have been arranged to overcome the barriers, would this type of person reflect significant personal change?

See also Bower (1973); Kauffmann (1982); Carlson et al. (1990).

7. See Billigmeier and Forman (1975); Carsello and Greiser (1976); Pelowski (1979); Davies (1974); Nash (1976); James (1976); Price and Hensley (1978); Pfnister (1979); Kauffmann (1982); Koester (1985).

8. For Nash (1976), autonomy means self-determination or personal freedom. For Abrams and Arnold (1967), autonomy refers to the qualities of independence and self-reliance.

9. Nash (1976) uses the Rosenberg Self-Evaluation Scale to assess changes in self-confidence. Hensley and Sell (1979) use the same scale for assessing changes in what they call self-esteem.

10. Churchill states that if changes are to persist, the following conditions need to be met on return: (1) students need to report experience, (2) students need to exchange experiences and impressions with others who have been abroad, and (3) students need to achieve some recognition of the value of both cultures.

CHAPTER FIVE

EDUCATION AS CHANGE

In this chapter we present an integrative, developmental model for understanding the impact study abroad has on students as discussed in the first four chapters. This model also provides a framework for interpreting the contradictions between student reports and the empirical research on effects of study abroad.

The model represents a new paradigm for measuring the personal growth and learning that occurs during the study abroad experience. Most importantly, it assumes that human maturation depends upon the quality of the interaction between individuals and their environments.

For students abroad who are involved in experiencing a new culture, personal growth and academic learning tend to flow together. This leads to a way of knowing that changes their thinking and behavior. Our model shows, in an integrated manner, how these personal and academic changes are interrelated.

Finally, we suggest that study abroad is the prototype for a new perspective in education, a new approach to learning that is holistic, synergistic, and multifaceted, that cannot be understood or measured by conventional reductionistic approaches. Study abroad challenges educators and researchers to discover new ways to explain and measure the process of change that is called "education."

True education means change. Brueggemann (1987), reflecting on individual personal development, asserts that changes in individuals occur in periods of discontinuity, displacement, and disjunction. New insights and revelations occur at points of disjunction, not in situations of equilibrium. "Personal development is ... about ... interaction in which the person is evoked, assaulted, and impinged upon in formative and transformative ways.... " (9).

Piaget and Inhelder (1958) viewed change as the essence of the maturation process, suggesting that as persons, our view of reality expands when we experience discrepancy between what we already understand and what our environment presents to us. Resolution of this discrepancy transforms the previous view of how objects and events are related into a new and more mature understanding. In this way individuals, in interaction with the environment, develop increasingly complex capacities to perceive and interact with their world.

He goes on to describe change as a complex, evolving process of balancing and rebalancing, of assimilation and accommodation. Assimilation involves interpreting a new experience in terms of current or previous structures of knowledge. Accommodation involves modifying existing ways of looking at the world to incorporate new knowledge or experience. Assimilation represents continuity; accommodation represents change. When individuals are only assimilating, they can become very bored. On the other hand when too much accommodation is required, they can become stressed. Human beings seek an equilibrium between the two. Development, then, is an evolving process of moving from equilibrium through disequilibrium toward a new equilibrium.

Sharon Parks (1986, 39) extends Piaget's central insights to a larger theory of self. She asserts that the dynamic of change not only affects how we understand the world but the development of our whole personality.[1] This view of change assumes that human maturation depends entirely upon the quality of the interaction between individuals and their environments. People do not mature in a vacuum.

Interaction with the environment is subtle and complex. According to Charles Schroeder (1984), human development is a function of person/environment interaction mediated by an appropriate ratio between challenge and support. Challenge often results from diversity and freedom in the environment, while support results from structure, personal guidance, and careful instruction. If an environment has been overly supportive, students may be satisfied but not adequately challenged to grow. If an environment is overly challenging, students may be so overwhelmed and overstimulated that development will not occur. In order to work with an individual's needs, styles and aptitudes, this ratio between challenge and support must always be considered.

Living abroad is a powerful environment for self-transformation. Students grow in their perceptions of themselves and the world and in the ways they compose meaning. They are challenged to account in new ways for things they are observing, because the old ways of viewing self and the world are no longer adequate.

A foreign culture places a student in a new and unfamiliar setting. Customs that were at home merely matters of assimilation—foods eaten, transportation used, religious and family customs—become matters of accommodation as the students are required to recompose their habits and ways of looking at the world.[2]

But living abroad is an agent for change not only because of the unfamiliar setting but also because it forces a change in the students' network of belonging, as noted by Parks and illustrated by student interviews in this book. The students' new social constellation abroad frees them to ask questions and reshape their self-images. This reshaping would be difficult back home, where they would be considered "out of bounds" by their peer groups, and their acceptance would thereby be threatened.

In this chapter we explain more precisely how students change during study abroad, from a personal, developmental perspective. We present a model drawn from theoretical literature which provides a framework for interpreting student reports of the various effects of study abroad. We also discuss why much of the empirical research has not systematically documented these reported changes.

A MODEL OF THE TRANSFORMATION PROCESS

The central insight from Piaget and others is that personal development is stimulated by the interaction between the person and his or her environment, between self and world. According to current research on study abroad, this interaction is mediated by six variables, all discussed in earlier chapters:

1. Autonomy (chapter 4)
2. Belonging (chapter 4)
3. Values (chapter 4)
4. Cognition (chapter 2)
5. Vocation (chapter 4)
6. Worldview (chapter 3)

Woven together, these aspects of personality form a descriptive model of the journey to maturation. Although this model is drawn from the tools of social science, it finds resonance in the stories of those who have lived abroad.

Cognitive development—the process of acquiring knowledge—is the goal of a university education. Yet growth in cognition must go hand in hand with growth in the other aspects of personality. The model outlined below (figure 1) represents a pattern of development from adolescence to adulthood. It demonstrates the interrelatedness between the cognitive and noncognitive aspects of personality. In this chapter we will look at how the study abroad experience stimulates change in each of these aspects of personality.

FIGURE 1

autonomy	belonging	values	cognition/ vocation	worldview
Level I other-dependent	conventional — diffuse	inherited	dualistic	encapsulated ethnocentrism
Level II inner-dependent	self-selected group	searching	relativistic	empathic ethnorelativism
Level III inter-dependent	open	owned	commitment in relativism	integrated ethnorelativism

AUTONOMY

Autonomy refers to the way one person relates to another. According to Parks (1986),

> humans are always and necessarily interdependent beings, but the form, experience, and awareness of dependence changes . . . .This aspect of the personality touches the core of the self so profoundly that emotions such as confidence, fear, vulnerability, and strength are inevitably evoked—emotions that undergo transformation and development (54).

The move from *other-dependency* to *inner-dependency* generally occurs in late adolescence and the early twenties. In adolescence, a dependent person's sense of the world resides in an uncritically assumed authority outside of the self. At this stage, parents, teachers, ministers, or others serve as mediators of the truth.

One form of dependency is *counter-dependence,* where the desire for more independence is often expressed by moving in the opposite direction of those who have been in authority. When authority figures say yes, the counter-dependent person says no, and vice versa. Even though this represents a strand of authority-bound dependency, it is a move toward another level of autonomy.

As one matures and reaches the inner-dependent stage, other sources of authority are still very important, but one begins to value the authority of the self as well, assuming the responsibility for deciding which authority is to be taken seriously.[3]

While some young adults may begin to experience some forms of interdependence, Parks believes that most people make the transition to the third level, *interdependence,* in the midlife years. Only then can a deeper understanding and trust of the self allow a "more profound awareness of one's relatedness to others" (59). At this stage, trust is centered in the meeting of self and other, and in recognizing the strength of each.

Many students report that they are more autonomous after living abroad, reflecting progress toward inner-dependence as a result of their experience. Consistent with research mentioned in the previous chapter, our model predicts that students who are at the other-dependent level of autonomy before departure will more likely report positive changes than will those who are already inner-dependent. However, the inner-dependent students are more ready to deal with the complexities of the new culture and have more capacity to alter their thinking, values, and view of the world than those who are less mature.

It should be noted, however, that if interdependence is really only experienced in the fullest sense at midlife, then one cannot expect young adults to be fully at that level of development, regardless of the richness of the study abroad environment.

This column of the model helps us understand why changes in self-confidence and self-esteem are reported by many returning study abroad students. A positive change in the level of autonomy most likely results in positive changes in self-understanding, self-confidence, self-esteem, and self-reliance.

Of all the students interviewed who reported significant personal change, Deb illustrated most clearly a person transformed from dependence on external authority to inner-dependence. Prior to her experience in Costa Rica, she wanted to become more inner-dependent but said she was "too afraid to let go of the past."

> I was holding on to my parents and others in very dependent ways. Just being down in Costa Rica has moved me. I now have the courage to be independent. I am now more my own person. Costa Rica gave me the courage to do what I wanted to do for so long. . . . I still have a lot of stress, but I just feel like I am more prepared to graduate and move on.

Don, Mike, Bob, Beth, and other students reported similar steps toward inner-dependence. Mike illustrated this progress when he described how he began to trust his own ability to make decisions and get around the city on his own.

> I started to realize that I could do things myself. I didn't have to be part of a group that went into town. I could go into town by myself. I went to look at art museums and took off on other types of field trips on my own. The fact that I did it without having a whole bunch of people with me made me feel pretty good.

BELONGING

While the levels of maturity are often measured in terms of degrees of autonomy and individuation, maturation is actually intertwined with belonging and with relationships. Parks (1986) has caught this connection when she says

> the motion of meaning-making is located in the oscillation between "two great yearnings" of human beings: the yearning to be distinct—to exercise one's own action in the world, to stand alone, to differentiate the self from the other—and the yearning for connection, inclusion, belonging, relation, intimacy and communion (63).

In Western cultures in particular, where individuality is a standard for maturity, the role of personal relationships and belonging is obscured, or even viewed as a sign of immaturity (63). Yet, the capacity to forge effective connections and interactions with other people—to build a "network of belonging"—is very important in understanding ultimate reality. "The human being does not compose meaning all alone. The individual person is not the sole actor in the drama of human development" (61). One of the important factors in developing effective connections is the capacity not simply to tolerate but to appreciate differences in other people, groups, and cultures.

As individuals mature, the shape of their relationships with others changes. "We never outgrow our need for others, but what others mean to us undergoes transformation" (63). Parks identifies four forms of community along the pathway to adulthood: *conventional, diffuse self-selected group,* and *open* to others.

An adolescent at the level of conventional groupings

conforms to class norms and interests. A person belongs simply by being born into the group or by reason of other circumstances. These groups are defined by ethnic-familial ties, class norms, regional perspectives and loyalties, religious systems, peer values and pressures, and gender. This form of belonging corresponds to the other-dependent level of autonomy.

As young adults gain more autonomy, they must confront new questions about the boundaries of relationships. At this stage, their connections are diffuse. They explore and experiment and are tentative about relationships, feeling that one sort of relationship may be as good as any other. Sustaining any particular relationship is problematic because it might cut off new possibilities. Still, the young person realizes that other people are essential to his or her search for a new pattern of knowing and being in the world, and so moves on to the next level: identifying with a self-selected group. This reflects a new perception of the world. The self-selected group represents an expansion of previously held boundaries of family, ethnicity, and geography and is composed of "those who count" or are "of like mind."

This new group seems better able to confirm and support newly required patterns of understanding self and the world. Students who return from studying abroad tend to form new patterns of affiliation upon their return. The new form of community, a self-selected group, is likely to take shape with those who have also traveled abroad, or at least with those who view the world and compose meaning in a similar way.

The ongoing encounter with others in the world requires continual recomposing of what is true of the self in relationship with others. Eventually some students at level two begin to be aware that a "self-selected group" may not be adequately inclusive of others and their perspectives. This challenge to their awareness fosters movement to the next form of community, one that is truly open to others. (While some young adults make this transition, most people do so at midlife.)

This form of community represents an advance in inclusiveness and is identified by commitment "to inclusive community marked by justice and love" (Parks 1986, 68). This is an alliance with those that are truly other than oneself—those that see the world differently. Community formed of those of critical but like mind, as in a self-selected form of community, may in fact represent a diminished openness to others. True openness to others challenges a system that protects the rights of some people while neglecting the rights of others.

College students tend to be working their way out of level one toward level two of the community continuum. The spur that the study abroad experience gives to this process is one of its values. In Costa Rica, Phil observed changing levels of belonging within his group of Goshen students. For him, the transition toward more diffuse relationships began there.

> For some, this is a beginning of learning some social skills. For others who have had these skills it is a continuation but not as central to the experience. Also, when you are down there, everybody is relying on everybody else. We eat lunch with different people all the time. Here on campus I always eat with the same two guys. It was good to be with different people. I think it would be a detriment to the group to have too many good friends because [that] splits [the group] up. It is funny because some of the people that I thought would end up driving me nuts turned out to be a lot of fun, and some others that I thought wouldn't, ended up doing so. One of the guys that I thought was loud and obnoxious and that I thought I would never like—I really got to know and appreciate. I really love the guy; we had a lot of fun.

When Jennifer left the Goshen College campus to go to China, her network of belonging was diffuse. Upon her return she built a network of belonging that was more self-selected.

> I was with a wide variety of people my freshman year, and I knew I couldn't be with them all in the future. SST helped me to narrow the focus—it was my clearly seeing who I was and being able to disclose that to others. That allows others to choose or reject a relationship with me and for me to feel good about it.

VALUES

The development of values, like the other aspects of personality, appears to offer its own path to maturity. Westerhoff (1976) proposes a schema in describing faith development that is useful in understanding the development of values in general, as shown in figure 1. He identifies four styles (ways of behaving) of faith: (1) experienced faith, (2) affiliative faith, (3) searching faith, and (4) owned faith. Each style is viewed as a whole in itself and at the same time as a sequence, each successive style building upon and incorporating the previous dominant style. Experienced faith is dominant in childhood while the affiliative faith style is dominant during the school years in which one learns the story of his/her nurturing community. With the further development of faith there follows a period of searching faith, marked by a time of questioning, experimentation, acting out against the community, and commitments to various ideologies. Late adolescence and young adulthood appear to be the usual time for the development of searching faith. When the needs of these three styles of faith have been met, an owned faith may develop as a dominant style.

In the model (figure 1) the term *inherited* is used as a

descriptor for those students at the first level of values development. This term is meant to include both the experienced and the affiliative styles of faith/values development. It also seems to describe more geographically the dominant theme of students entering college—students who have done very little personal reflection on their own faith/values development.

Their political, religious, and other preferences are those of their parents, home community, or some other authority figure. Those who enter a study abroad program with a largely inherited set of values will probably be forced to examine these values during a phase of questioning and searching and to decide which to make their own and which to discard.

This period of *searching* corresponds to the progression from dependency to inner-dependency and from the conventional form of belonging to one in which group identities are selected. It is a time in which students often feel that one set of values is as good as any other, that any belief, no matter how sacred, is up for evaluation. For example, those who were formerly very religious may at this stage raise questions about the existence of God. Those who believed that American democracy was the ultimate political good may begin to question its perfection. At this stage, choices related to values are held in abeyance—to make a choice for one set of values means the rejection of others, implying that they are wrong.

Developing a new set of values takes time, but it is almost inevitable for study abroad students as they are confronted with different ways of thinking and believing. In this phase, they decide to retain certain inherited values, revise others, and possibly adopt new ones.

For example, when Don arrived in Costa Rica, he discovered that relationships with people seemed to be more important than efficiency and making money. People seemed to live happily without the luxuries he was used to. He reports that he seriously evaluated and then restructured the values he inherited. He no longer "has the desire to be rich no matter what it takes."

Denise's experience in China helped her to expand her horizons and to explore the core beliefs of her religious faith.

> I realized that a lot of what I tied to religion before I went didn't seem central at all when I was in China. When you tried to explain religion in terms of customs and things like that to the Chinese, it seemed ridiculous.... This experience shook some of my religious perspectives and strengthened what is central to my belief. Central to my conviction is that there is a God that can speak to all people and transcend culture. One thing that got turned around was the belief that Christianity is the only way ... of understanding God. Some of the truths of Confucianism [are] so similar that I would not write that off as being invalid.

For most students, study abroad expands the values options. Few will return ready to make commitments to values that are uniquely their own; still, many will have begun the journey.

COGNITION

Cognition refers to intellectual development. Based on extensive research of college students, William Perry (1970) has identified nine levels of intellectual development. Three levels are included in figure 1.

At the first level, adolescents' thinking is *dualistic* and is closely tied to the other-dependent form of autonomy, the conventional form of belonging and the inherited stage of value development. What this adolescent really knows is based on some external authority—a person or group. At this level, one makes clear delineations between right and wrong, truth and untruth, and who is included and who is not. To a large degree this is based on the conventional community within which the young person has grown up.

Movement from this uncritical, dualistic level is often brought on by experiences that cannot be assimilated into the old, established explanations. This leads the student to the next level, to believing that all truth is relative and that knowledge is conditioned by the particularity of the context in which it is composed. This shift from authority-bound dualism to *relativism* is often fostered when a student begins associating with people who have new ways of defining truth. The old ways of looking at the world no longer fit and new ways have to be found. At this level, students recognize that knowledge is contextual and relative. Different perspectives are acknowledged and these perspectives are seen as pieces that fit together into a larger whole.

However, complete relativism is not permanent. After all, one needs to move on, to decide what is worthwhile and valuable for oneself, and, at the same time, accept the validity of different choices made by other people. This level of development is referred to as *commitment in relativism.*

To make a commitment in relativism is to make a self-conscious choice for one's way of knowing. Students who arrive at this level of knowing have made active affirmations of themselves and their responsibilities in a pluralistic world, establishing their identities in the process. Personal commitments in such areas as life-style, marriage/singleness, faith, or career are made out of a relativistic frame of reference.

It was readily apparent that the students interviewed were at various levels of cognitive development. Those who entered the experience from a dualistic framework were often quickly aware that their ways of knowing were inadequate.

Some who were relativistic upon departure were very open to the new perceptions of truth that they were encountering. A few began to try to decide what would be central for them.

Denise was a student who was open to new perspectives on truth when she went to China. She began to make the intellectual choices that would shape her view of religion. Elaborating on her comments on page 136, she said,

> Customs are a practice of how we interpret an understanding of God, and it becomes important to focus on universals and not try to force customs on others as a means of expression. While this experience shook some of my religious perspectives, it helped me sort out what is central to my belief. In the midst of many good perspectives on religion, I could choose to claim the conviction that there is a God that can speak to all people and transcend culture. This conviction may get altered as I gain new insight, but this is the conviction upon which I will operate until better insight comes to me.

VOCATION

Discovering a vocation means exploring, through the many aspects of the learning environment, what one's life is to be and how one wishes to serve humanity. Vocation is not simply an occupation or a career; it is that sense of purpose which occupies us—a summons to be our unique selves, a summons to do the work indicated by the human context to which we are committed.

In previous chapters we noted that, contrary to conventional wisdom, students do not tend to narrow their vocational options through study abroad. Instead, most return with an expanded range of options for their place in society. Two researchers, Knefelkamp and Sleptiza (1976, 53–58), helped explain this by adapting Perry's cognitive model to produce a cognitive-developmental model for vocational development. They suggest that vocational maturity level is very closely linked to the cognitive developmental level of the student. For example, students who use simplistic, dualistic thinking believe that one right vocation exists which somehow needs to be discovered (someone can surely give me the right answer). Vocational choices are either provided by the career counselor (or some other authority figure) or by some vocational test.

Many times students abroad begin to realize that the simple approach (dualistic) to vocational decision making is inadequate. They move to a more relativistic view of vocation as their experience opens up new options. What had originally appeared to be a simple and clear process for making a career choice is now viewed as much more complex and in some cases overwhelming. Majors and career choices may be postponed or radically altered. How does one choose a college major in light of the new uncertainty? Other career possibilities may be so appealing that it becomes difficult to select—choosing one may eliminate another avenue that some day might prove to be a better direction than the one selected.

Making a commitment to one vocational choice from numerous options (commitment in relativism) is yet to come. Narrowing to one vocational choice takes further processing time, depending on the individual. Tim, a student in Goshen College's Study Service Term in Germany, illustrated well how an experience abroad can foster change in vocational development. He is moving closer to the final stage.

> Because of my SST experience I changed my major. I was a business major before I left, but as a result of my experience in Germany, I decided to go with an education major and a business minor. I decided

> that teaching is something that I would really enjoy, not only for the things I would get out of it but also for what I could give to the students. I want to keep my options open for business too.... Maybe in the future I could go into secondary education, but right now I feel I should go into elementary education. I might feel enough unchallenged that I will go on in a master's program and qualify to teach secondary later.

WORLDVIEW

The term *worldview* suggests some sort of major unifying perception (Ong 1969). It refers to our personal perceptions of "what is and how it is" (4). A worldview "defines, organizes, and brings order to [our] lives" (Newton and Caple 1985, 163).

Individuals who are at the first level of development (dependent, with conventional networks of belonging, who process information simplistically and hold largely inherited values) will probably be highly ethnocentric and have an *encapsulated* worldview. Augsburger (1986), paraphrasing an old proverb, said, "Anyone who knows only one culture knows no culture" (18).

For individuals at this level there is no other way to know reality from their perspective. The local is viewed as universal, the relative as absolute, and the complex as simple.

To move from encapsulation to empathic ethnorelativism, such a person will probably need more than traditional classroom learning to force change. New experiences and new encounters are required. As Augsburger put it,

> Nothing dissolves old assumptions like salt water, particularly crossing a large amount of it and finding oneself in a totally unfamiliar situation. Acceler-

> ated learning and unlearning occur as one discovers the immediate need to discard old givens and assimilate new options (25).

Milton Bennett (1986a) suggests that a "paradigmatic barrier" stands between the ethnocentric stage of development and the next stage of ethnorelativism. "Movement to the next stage represents a major conceptual shift from reliance on absolute principles of some sort to an acknowledgment of non-absolute relativity" (59). This new stage represents a major change in the meaning attributed to difference. In the ethnocentric state, difference is experienced as threatening, and actions taken in this state are meant to counter the threat in various ways. A person shifting to the new state of ethnorelativism will experience difference as nonthreatening. Cultural difference will more likely be viewed as enjoyable and welcomed.

According to Augsburger and Bennett, students can "cross over" into another culture and begin to have an empathic understanding for its people when they can temporarily put aside their own beliefs and enter the new culture's world of assumptions, beliefs, and values. Empathy represents a relatively high level of intercultural sensitivity.

As with the searching stage of values and the relativistic stage of cognition/vocation, the empathic stage of ethnorelativism is characterized by the nonevaluation of difference. But as Bennett points out, "cultural openness has a price—the paralysis of commitment" (59). Partially developed ethnorelativism may lead individuals into a "liberal quagmire," where all possible choices among alternative perspectives seem equally good. Experiencing this debilitating ambiguity over a long period may result in a retreat to the surer ground of ethnocentrism or into the mentally unstable conditions of "multiphrenia" or "detachment."

The person who truly crosses over into another culture

comes back a different person and looks at the world with fresh eyes. The change toward a bicultural or multicultural worldview takes place in the integration of new perspectives into old values and views. Integration allows for ethical choice and actions in the profoundly relativistic world by an ethnorelativistic identity.

Part of the reason reentry has been difficult for study abroad students is that they have not yet incorporated changes into their lives back in the States. They can no longer live as they had prior to the experience abroad, but their new selves do not fit comfortably into the old setting. The interviews with students illustrate this dramatically. As Bob, after his return from France, observed:

> This last year has been one of the most difficult in my life. Not that I want to go back to France, but returning home required a major reorientation for me, as I think it does for most people who study abroad. One of the things that should be emphasized for people on return is that there are counseling services that are available to them. I knew two women who went abroad the same year as I. I saw one of them in the mental health clinic the other day, and the other one I've talked to a few times. We are all having a really difficult time coming back.

SUMMARY OF THE MODEL

What emerges from our examination of the model is that students who are at level one prior to their experience abroad will tend to experience more personal change than those who are at level two. That is, they will likely return as more inner-dependent, likely to experiment with new networks of relationships, will be in search of their own values, will process information less simplistically, and will have broadened their worldview considerably.

Students who were at level two prior to departure, while experiencing personal growth, will not likely fully reach level-three behaviors and perspectives until their postcollege years. They will, however, reflect greater gains in the area of worldview/international perspective, as discussed in chapter 3.

IMPLICATIONS OF THE MODEL

The preceding model represents a different way of understanding, knowing, teaching, and learning. The inability of empirical research to adequately measure the changes described by students who have studied abroad may be the result of an inadequate educational paradigm.

Students abroad who are involved in the life of their host culture cannot separate out the personal from the academic. Involvement in the new culture draws the students in, and it leads them to a way of knowing that changes how they think and behave. This new knowledge cannot be held at arm's length, divorced from their personal lives. Students insist that immersion does not permit them to be merely spectators or to learn only at the cognitive level. It would appear that the intertwining of the academic and the personal has remained hidden to researchers using standardized instruments, which goes far in explaining the discrepancy between the results of the standardized "objective" evaluation tools and self-report data. The standardized instruments are based on the conventional educational model (a model that assumes a dualism between the cognitive and the affective realms) that might more accurately reflect traditional, campus-based educational results than those of study abroad. To be sure, many objectives of study abroad programs are conventionally based, but the problem is that actual outcomes often differ from the stated ones. Students express frustration with the evaluation instruments which fail to identify some of what they perceive to be the deeper and richer outcomes of studying abroad.

In a recent monograph, Kuh, Whitt, and Shedd (1987) discuss the emergence of a new paradigm of education, a new way of thinking about education. One of the characteristics of this transition is a shift from an overall perspective influenced by a reductionist, objectivist scientism to one that is more complex, relational, and context bound.

Parker Palmer (1987) suggests that there are promising movements toward this new perspective in today's intellectual world. The underlying theme in these new movements is relatedness. He cites feminist thought, African-American scholarship, and Native-American studies as examples of this shift. He says that in reading their history, "you are reading another kind of history, history that refuses to allow you to divorce your own story from the story being told" (2).

If study abroad represents a new way of knowing, then the means by which we evaluate this way of knowing will have to change. Evaluation from a single perspective (psychology, anthropology) is inadequate. Questionnaires using existing scales such as the Likert scale and standardized instruments like personality inventories place narrow constraints on what students can report. The changes experienced by students who study abroad have eluded simple interpretation.

We suggest that study abroad is the prototype for a new perspective in education, a new approach to learning that is holistic, synergistic, and multifaceted, and that cannot be understood or measured by conventional reductionistic approaches (Mestenhauser 1985, 133–82). Study abroad challenges educators and researchers to discover new ways to explain and measure the process of change that is the essence of education.

NOTES

1. Parks draws from a number of scholars, including Robert Kegan, Carol Gilligan, William Perry, and James Fowler.
2. Parks (1986) states, "Here in the dialectic between cultures, and at the level of basic physical nourishment, we experience development as it always presents itself—in the tension between self-preservation and self-transformation" (35).
3. "Inner dependence occurs when one is able to self-consciously include the self within the area of authority" (Parks 1986, 58).

CHAPTER SIX

STUDY ABROAD AND INTERNATIONALIZATION OF THE UNIVERSITY: RECOMMENDATIONS FOR ACTION

In this chapter we give specific recommendations for developing study abroad programs. These recommendations are related to foreign language learning, general studies requirements, enrichment of the students' majors, maintenance of the quality of study abroad programs, and reintegration of returning students.

American colleges and universities are faced with the question of how they should change to make learning relevant to the rapid internationalization of society and culture that has occurred in the last forty years. Study abroad is one of the most powerful tools available to educators to assist students in becoming educated people in today's interrelated world.

In chapter 5 we considered education as change, involving a balance between *assimilation* (interpreting a new experience in terms of current structures of knowing) and *accommodation* (modifying existing ways of knowing to incorporate new information or experience). We saw that when students spend time in foreign environments, they are confronted with knowledge and experience that do not fit their previous frames of reference. They must move beyond assimilation to accommodation. Study abroad is therefore a powerful stimulus to modify the ways they view the world.

Three of the four areas in which significant change occurs during study abroad are also part of the clearly defined mission of most university study abroad programs: foreign language competence, cognitive learning, and development of an international perspective. It is therefore clear that colleges and universities can both pursue their traditional goals in study abroad programming and at the same time foster growth in areas which are perceived by some as academically peripheral but which, in fact, are legitimate educational goals and constitute the most effective way to prepare students to function in the global society. Careful development of programs abroad is an institutional imperative if the college or university is to remain relevant in the world in which we now live. Let us examine more fully how institutions might enrich learning abroad in each of these three areas.

FOREIGN LANGUAGES MUST BE TAKEN SERIOUSLY

Every college graduate should have the ability to communicate in at least one foreign language. The failures of academic institutions in this realm are well known. Language is often seen as only a technical skill and is not taken seriously. Instructors are frequently teaching assistants or lecturers who are not in tenure-track positions, thus reflecting the low priority of foreign language courses. In addition, language learning is often simply a part of the first two years of a literature major; the goal of language acquisition for communication purposes—written and oral—is often ignored. We assume that learning a foreign language should be part of the high school curriculum, but we do not require competence in a language for admission to college.

As Milton Bennett points out, languages are more than "simply different codes with which to communicate similar ideas" (1986a, 46). They are conveyers of culturally integrated worldviews. Genuine competence comes from use of the language for real communication in an environment where the language is indigenous to the culture.

We recommend that every institution of higher education

1. require language majors and students preparing to teach a language to spend a minimum of one year studying at a location where the language is the principal one used;
2. identify a foreign study site for every language taught by the institution;
3. require competence testing for the language used in any study abroad program; and
4. offer on-site instruction abroad for students with inadequate language skills who plan to study

abroad and for other students who need to gain competence.

GENERAL STUDIES PROGRAMS NEED TO INCLUDE STUDY ABROAD

In chapter 3 the development of an international perspective was defined as including (1) changes in the perception of the host culture, (2) changes in the perception of the home culture, and (3) changes in knowledge, affective responses, and behavior regarding the world beyond one's national boundaries. In other words, the development of an international perspective involves a modification of (or accommodation in) the way one views the world.

This is at the heart of general studies. Central to many proposed modifications of general studies programs in recent years has been an effort to help students develop a broader worldview. Non-Western studies, studies of world cultures, ethnic studies, and experiential involvement with different cultures have in recent years been common additions to general studies curricula and are consistent with the internationalization of the university. More colleges and universities should use study abroad as a major means of developing an international perspective for their students. All should find a way to make study abroad a viable option for general studies.

We recommend that

1. general studies requirements be constructed in such a way that credit earned abroad outside of the major, up to some reasonable limit, satisfy general studies requirements.
2. an appropriate study abroad program that would meet part of the general studies requirements be available to every undergraduate student.

As was pointed out in chapter 4, the maturity level of the student is an essential consideration in finding an appropriate program. Each student needs to find his or her worldview challenged so that accommodation takes place. For less developmentally mature students this accommodation will result in primarily personal change. For such change to take place, maximum immersion in the foreign culture must be provided. Programs with a focus on language learning or programs with an experiential emphasis may often be excellent choices for such students. Homestays should be a part of the programs if at all possible.

For more mature students an appropriate program needs to provide an adequate challenge of more sophisticated material related to international understanding. The level of approach that will affect the worldview of a less mature student may well bore the more mature student who can easily assimilate it into an existing worldview. For mature students, programs with a greater emphasis on conventional courses or with directed independent research may be the best choice.

3. better geographical balance be achieved in available study abroad programs. Programs from the United States send students primarily to industrialized Western countries, although the number of programs in less developed countries has increased substantially in recent years. With the majority of the world's population living in less developed nations and with the recent dramatic political rearrangements in Eastern Europe, it is imperative that Americans become acquainted with these cultures.

4. programs be set up on the home campus to assist students throughout their reentry process. This is especially important for students who are returning from their first overseas experience but is also desirable for other students.

MAJORS CAN BE ENRICHED BY STUDY ABROAD

In a recent address, Clark Kerr (1989) suggested a division of disciplines into three areas. First are areas with *world-wide uniformity* in the content of knowledge, such as chemistry, mathematics, and physics: scholars everywhere all know the same things. Second are areas of *intra-cultural similarity* of knowledge, such as political science, history, most other social sciences, and the humanities. In these disciplines scholars know many of the same things within their cultural area and little outside it. Finally, there are areas of *intra-national particularity*. Included in this category are social welfare, public administration, and education. Scholars in these fields know some of the same things within their own society and usually nothing outside it. In a cursory look through the catalogue of the University of California, Berkeley, he calculated that about 60 percent of the courses listed were in the first category, about 30 percent in the second, and 10 percent in the last.

It would seem to follow that for disciplines in the intra-cultural similarity of knowledge area an undergraduate major could be substantially enriched and new perspectives found in the major by studying that discipline in another country. Even students in the area of world-wide uniformity of knowledge can learn new approaches by studying the subject in a different national setting. For example, the late William M.

Mosher pointed out that it was no accident that penicillin was discovered by Sir Alexander Fleming, a British scientist who pursued his research to find out what killed his bacteria, rather than by an American, who would have simply tossed in some copper sulfate to kill the mold so he could get on with his work.

It is also imperative that work done in the major abroad be integrated with coursework at home to form a coherent program.

For studies abroad that are part of the major we recommend that

1. if the language of instruction abroad is not English, either (a) competency testing be used to insure that only students with language skills adequate for pursuing classroom work be accepted in the program or (b) the program abroad provide adequate instruction to bring the students to the appropriate level before their courses begin.

2. staff and courses at the host universities be fully acceptable to the sending university and department. For undergraduate study the best research universities in a given country may not always offer appropriate coursework. The highest priority must be placed on the availability of instruction at the proper level when host universities are selected. The curriculum must be carefully examined by a faculty member from the related department of the sending institution.

3. requirements for majors be adapted by students' home departments to accommodate the studies abroad. One excellent approach is that of the

European Community's ERASMUS plan in which professors from the sending and receiving departments meet together and mutually decide what course content will most benefit students abroad. Special courses can be devised by the home department to be carried out abroad that will greatly enrich the U.S. curriculum.

4. American institutions use special care in selecting participants for programs. Two factors need attention: maturity and scholarly performance.

   It was pointed out earlier that students who are developmentally less mature do not achieve as high a level of international understanding as more mature students. We are not aware of definitive research that indicates a relationship between maturity and general scholarship, but in the absence of contrary evidence it seems reasonable to expect that the more mature student or the student who has been abroad previously would be less distracted by personal adjustments and therefore should do better in academic pursuits.

   The studies of grade point averages before, during, and after study abroad reported in chapter 2 would seem to indicate that for a mature student, performance in previous work at the home university is the best predictor of ability to do academic studies in a foreign university. The commonly accepted practice of requiring a given GPA for admittance to programs involving study in foreign universities seems well advised.

MAINTAINING QUALITY IN STUDY ABROAD

Colleges and universities have a commitment to produce graduates who have both an expanded way of looking at the world and who have acquired a body of knowledge. In the American system progress toward these goals is measured by the accumulation of credits. Therefore, academic work taken during foreign study needs to be translated into credits which meet the standards set by American accrediting agencies.

Differences between the U.S. system of education and the systems of other countries often make it difficult for students to pursue academic work with the same intensity they would at home. As an example, we reported in chapter 2 the results of the SAEP study (Carlson et al. 1990) in which students judged the foreign universities to be weaker in organization of classes and lectures and in evaluation and frequency of assignments. This often means that the U.S. college or university needs to find ways to insure that its students are self-motivated and able to function in the new system.

Attention to quality is equally important when the overseas program is an extension of the home institution. Faculty abroad are often vulnerable to being so impressed with the personal development they see in students that they fail to ensure that cognitive learning is maximized.

In order to maintain acceptable academic standards in study abroad programs we recommend that

1. students have access to the literature pertinent to their studies and that the program require them to utilize it. Adequate library facilities need to be arranged. If the focus of a program is narrow, it may be satisfactory to develop a special library for the students. If the long-range goal is

to produce scholars who can pursue studies in the area in the future, it is a good investment to help students learn to use local library facilities even though the time required and process involved is more cumbersome.

2. study abroad programs develop ways to assure that students engage in reflective analysis of what they experience. This is a time in their lives when they are experiencing major dislocations relative to their ideas and their values and assumptions. The balance between assimilating experiences and new ideas into the existing worldview and expanding that view to accommodate new material is crucial. This may be done by required papers, journals, and faculty-led group discussions.

3. appropriate evaluation of the student's work be made. If the work is directed by an American professor, the usual instruments of evaluation can easily be employed. If the work is taken under the direction of a foreign professor, some means for translating the evaluation to the U.S. system needs to be devised.

4. the amount of credit be carefully controlled. There is a strong tendency for professors to feel the students are making so much more progress than they would have at home (and often they are) that they deserve credit just for being abroad. Under systems that involve more individual effort and independent initiative, such as the British system, counting class hours to determine the amount of credit makes no sense. How-

ever, the Carnegie Rule that says a maximum of one semester hour (or 1-1/2 quarter hours) of credit should be earned in a week of study is expected to apply to study abroad programs.

REINTEGRATING STUDENTS INTO HOME INSTITUTIONS

A common complaint of study abroad students is the difficulty they have in readjusting to life back home, academically as well as personally and socially. Many feel that their institutions do not recognize the significance of their overseas experience and even punish them for this deviation from their academic career. Students we interviewed reported that their newfound international skills were not recognized or utilized by their institutions and that there were no formal mechanisms to assist them in integrating their overseas learning with their on-campus instruction. It is well known that the significance of the overseas experience is not recognized and the full impact not realized without some deliberate reflection and examination.

In addition to reintegrating into academic life, returning students are at the same time readjusting to their family and social life—which has often changed during their time abroad. Many students find it is more difficult to readjust to life back home than it was to adjust to a foreign culture, partly because this readjustment is so unexpected. Most students and their friends and family are unaware of this "reverse culture shock" phenomenon.

In order to maximize the study abroad experience for both the student and the institution, and to facilitate the students' reentry, we recommend that

1. formal recognition of the value of the overseas experience be granted by the institution. This

may be done by insuring that credit for overseas work is awarded smoothly and efficiently. In addition, returning students should not be penalized for missing administrative deadlines such as financial aid deadlines and preregistration.

2. returned students be provided a forum for reporting their experiences and learning. This can be achieved in a number of ways, including a series of brown-bag seminars or travelogue nights, where groups of students report on their travels and study and a one- to three-credit reentry course that could be cross-listed in several departments (e.g., communication, anthropology, general studies).

3. the institution take advantage of students' newly acquired international expertise. Returned students should be incorporated into the administrative structure of the international programs, that is, sitting on boards that oversee international programs. Also, returning students should be asked to contribute to predeparture orientation for departing students or to orientation for incoming international students. Some of the most dynamic cross-cultural learning occurs between returned U.S. students and incoming international students.

4. the institution provide career and academic advisement that recognizes and incorporates new directions as a result of the overseas experience. Many students return from abroad with a conviction that they want to do "something international" as a career but are unclear about their

specific career path. The career office could provide information about careers with an international focus.

5. returning students be made aware of appropriate counseling services. Sometimes, advisors at the international student office may be better equipped to deal with these issues than the counseling centers. Cultural adjustment can be stressful, and services should be provided to facilitate this process.

6. the institution provide formal reentry workshops for returning students. Students can be guided to reflect on what they learned overseas, on how to incorporate this into their on-campus study, on how they may have changed personally, and on how to manage the reaction (or lack of one) they receive from family, faculty and peers.

Many of the recommendations here can be incorporated into a half- or whole-day workshop. By conducting such a workshop, the institution provides recognition of the importance of study abroad, and study abroad students will have opportunities to synthesize as well as share what they have gained from their overseas experience. Materials can be presented on international careers and further international study opportunities, and information can be presented about international opportunities on campus.

We hope these recommendations may assist faculty and administrators to debate the relevant issues as they design new programs for study abroad or revise existing ones. In many ways this form of education is in its infancy. We have shared here the results of studies about the effectiveness of such programs to date. In the appendix we have summarized the research and in so doing suggest additional areas for further study. It is important that all involved in the operation of programs abroad engage in continual evaluation of their efforts. We hope that in the next few years more research on and evaluation of innovative programing can lead to significant advances in making study abroad a standard part of a university education. We believe that it is one of the most powerful tools of education available to prepare students to be not strangers, but leaders, both at home and in our global society.

APPENDIX

Table 1

Synthesis of Salient Findings from Research about Study Abroad Which Used Existing Instruments

Researcher (year), College and Location	*Sample*	*Instrumentation*
McGuigan (1958) Hollins College Study Abroad Program in 1955–56, 1956–57	N=49 (2 experimental groups) N=104 (control groups)	(1955–56): 1. Study of Values 2. Security-Insecurity Inventory 3. Bogardus Scale of Social Distance 4. World-mindedness Scale (1956–57) (as above) 5. Eight personality inventories
McGuigan (1959) another Hollins College sample		1. Social and Personal Distance Scale 2. Adorno's Authoritarian Scale 3. Pelmutter's Scale of Hostile Feelings toward Americans 4. Pelmutter's Xenophile Scale 5. Finley's Social Opinion Inventory 6. Navorani Dependency Scale
Leonard (1959) Adelphi College Western Europe	N=14 (no control group)	1. Allport-Vernon "Study of Values" 2. Adorno PEC (Political Economic Conservatism) 3. Subjective data, i.e., journals, essays

Appendix 1

Findings Related to Personal Change	*Personality Changes Linked to Specific Experience Abroad*
Only two significant findings: study abroad students reported higher social values and more tendency to conform	
Those who went abroad rated Americans less favorably and became significantly more xenophobic and dependent	
1. Increase in liberalization of attitudes	

Researcher (year), College and Location	*Sample*	*Instrumentation*
Kafka (1968) Justin Morrill College undergrads	N=81 (exp grp) N=127 (ctrl grp)	1. World-mindedness Scale 2. Dogmatism Scale 3. Differential Values
Smith, C.T. (1971) Kalamazoo College Africa, France Germany, Spain		Pre- and Post- 1. CEEB—Foreign Language Reading and Listening Test 2. Allport-Vernon-Lindzey Study of Values 3. ETS—college student questionnaire attitude scales 4. Locally designed self-perception questionnaire 5. Third-person ratings

Findings Related to Personal Change	*Personality Changes Linked to Specific Experience Abroad*
No variables related to change in world-mindedness; exposure to foreign culture reinforced appreciation for home country at expense of the nation visited	Those who achieved cross-cultural immersion: more frequent and more intimate contact with host nationals, more confidence in language ability; their ratings of host country improved at expense of the U.S.
Greater development of attitudes, values, and interests	More changes in attitudes, values, and interests associated with the following organizational and structural characteristics: 1. Breadth of exposure to non-Americans 2. The presence of American subculture 3. Living with host families 4. Instruction in English versus total instruction in language of host culture

Researcher (year), College and Location	*Sample*	*Instrumentation*
Stauffer (1973) Otterbein College in Sierra Leone, West Africa	N=15	1. Teacher's Situation Reaction Test (TSRT) 2. Teacher's Career Survey (TCS) 3. Interviews with students and instructors
Hoeh and Spuck (1975) South Side High School Grosse Pointe, Michigan France	N=15	1. Semantic Differentials of Attitudes toward Self and French People (SEMDIF) 2. Student Attitude toward Life in France (SATLIF)
Hensley and Sell (1979) Kent State Geneva, Switzerland	N=52 N=17 (ctrl grp)	Likert-type instruments 1. Rosenberg—for self-acceptance aspect of self-esteem 2. Budner—tolerance of ambiguity
Pyle (1981) Alma College Woburn Lawn, Jamaica	N=22 (exp grp) N=14 (ctrl grp)	1. Interviews 2. SDTI (Student Development Task Inventory)

Appendix 1

Findings Related to Personal Change	*Personality Changes Linked to Specific Experience Abroad*
Conceptual and experiential gains in cross-cultural understanding and the attendant discovery of self in the development of new empathies	
Positive change in self-concept	
Students' level of self-esteem tended to increase	Extent of contact with non-Americans
1. Increased autonomy, especially in independence 2. Mature lifestyle 3. Very positive attitudes toward experience	

Appendix 1

Researcher (year), College and Location	*Sample*	*Instrumentation*
Kauffmann (1982)	N = 126	1. OPI (Omnibus Personality Inventory) 2. Debriefing Interview Guide
Carlson and Widaman (1988) University of Colorado, Boulder; University of Massachusetts, Amherst; Kalamazoo College; University of California undergrads	N = 450 former study abroad students N = 800 (ctrl grp)	Questionnaire on attitudes related to international understanding, adapted from Barrows (1981) instrument
Carlson, Burn, Useem, Yachimowicz (1990) (Same as above)	Same as above	Same

Findings Related to Personal Change	*Personality Changes Linked to Specific Experience Abroad*
1. Increased interest in reflective thought 2. Increased self-esteem and independence 3. Increased interest in the welfare of others	1. Depth of contact with culture 2. Service assignment 3. National homes
Study abroad group showed higher levels in cross-cultural interest, cultural cosmopolitanism, and international political concern; study abroad group also reported more positive and also more critical attitudes toward the U.S.	
Further analysis of data (reconfiguring of factors): study abroad group higher in peace and cooperation factor, cross-cultural interest, and respect—both before and after study abroad; neither control nor study abroad group increased significantly between pre- and poststudy abroad; no differences for international concern factor	
U.S. students were more positive toward some aspects of the U.S. and more negative toward others	

Researcher (year), College and Location	*Sample*	*Instrumentation*
Carlson, Burn, Useem, Yachimowicz (1990)	N = 301	1. ETS Self-Appraisal 2. ACTFL Oral Proficiency
(Same as above)		

Appendix 1

Findings Related to Personal Change	Personality Changes Linked to Specific Experience Abroad
In France, Germany, and Sweden students from intermediate to advanced level of language	
The more time students spent with other Americans, the less the increase in their language skills	
Compared to the U.S., students ranked academic experience expected of Americans as lower in Germany and France and about the same in Sweden and the United Kingdom	
Sixty-six percent of students took courses abroad not available at home	
Students ranked their general intellectual development higher abroad than it would have been at home	
Students who gained the most from nonacademic pursuits had superior academic performance	
Students' level of knowledge about host country increased dramatically as a result of living and studying abroad	
Sixty-eight percent of students took courses to broaden their academic and cultural backgrounds	
After being abroad, students considered getting good grades and learning facts less important than before	

TABLE 2
Synthesis of Salient Findings from Research about Study Abroad Which Used Specially Designed Instruments

Researcher (year), College and Location	*Sample*	*Instrumentation*
Smith, H.P. (1955) Experiment in International Living homestay group; National Student Association tourists; Quaker International Voluntary Service worker	N=310 (4 exp grps) N=64 (ctrl grps)	1. World-Mindedness Scale 2. California Public Opinion Scale (Ethnocentrism, Fascism, & Political-Economic Conservatism Scales) 3. Democracy Scale
Smith, H.P. (1957) follow-up of 1955 study (same group as above)	N=205 (4 exp grps) N=10 (ctrl grp)	Same as 1955 questions about previous experience and activities since 1955 study
Pace (1959) University of Delaware, Sweet Briar College in France	N=500 Self-selected sample drawn from all participants from 1923–1953	Questionnaire Six subscales to measure openness and attitudes

Appendix 2

Findings Related to Personal Change	*Personality Changes Linked to Specific Experience Abroad*
1. Little overall attitude change in sojourners 2. Conclusion that existing attitudes very important 3. Positive change for those sojourning in England 4. Increased international activity for those who formed close intercultural relationships	Type of contact Preexisting attitudes
1. No changes in internationally oriented behavior 2. Students became less world-minded, less ethnocentric, less authoritarian and more conservative (recent events affect attitudes more than intercultural travel)	Preexisting attitudes
1. Personally more tolerant in acceptance of people who differ from themselves 2. More inclined to endorse policies which promote the freer exchange of ideas, goods, and people among nations	

Researcher (year), College and Location	*Sample*	*Instrumentation*
Burnham, Trendler, and Harris (1966)	N = 20	Interview of students upon return
Hoffman and Zak (1969) U.S. and Canadian Jewish campers	N = 112 (2 ctrl grps)	Attitude instrument adapted from Herman 1970 reported in Sell 1983
Pfnister (1972) Goshen College Evaluation of students studying in Third-World countries	N = 120 (2 ctrl grps)	In-depth interviews
Davies (1974) liberal arts college students in Midwest	N = 105	1. Individual opinion inventory 2. Scholastic aptitude (Form A) a. Foreign Language Test b. Math and Verbal
Marion (1974) University of Colorado programs in Western Europe	N = 90	1. Antecedent questionnaire 2. Transactions questionnaire 3. Attitude scales: internationalism, open/close-mindedness, radicalism, conservatism, self-assessment, perception of host country, perception of U.S.

Appendix 2

Findings Related to Personal Change	*Personality Changes Linked to Specific Experience Abroad*
A majority of students reported changes in academic plans, social interests, political viewpoints	
High-contact group became more favorable in attitude	Degree of contact
Increased tolerance and understanding of other people and their views	
High scorers in "development of the individual person" correlated positively with international study	Positive experience related to individual development
Students became significantly less positive toward host countries	

Researcher (year), College and Location	*Sample*	*Instrumentation*
Billigmeier and Forman (1975)	N=39	Questionnaire—evaluates academic, intellectual, cultural, and personal aspects of program
Salter and Teger (1975) Intervarsity Christian Fellowship (workers and tourists)	N=35 (2 exp grps) N=38 (2 ctrl grps)	Questionnaire—measures degree of positive feeling about host country (27 questions)
Carsello and Grieser (1976) Students from various U.S. colleges studying in Italy, France, Spain, and Switzerland	N=209	Questionnaire

Appendix 2

Findings Related to Personal Change	*Personality Changes Linked to Specific Experience Abroad*
1. Twelve indicated an immense interest and participation in the fine arts 2. More than 50 percent felt their values had been influenced by contact with host culture 3. Nineteen felt they had grown in the area of personal motivation (independence, self-reliance, ability to make decisions) 4. Fifty percent reported new perspectives and greater understanding of their host culture	
1. Travelers increased positive attitudes 2. Working sojourners decreased in positive attitudes 3. Host country also influenced positive/negative change in attitudes	Type of contact (genuine in-depth contact fostered change; no change associated with superficial contact), location of study abroad, and equal status were not found to be important factors
1. Increased interest in travel, art, foreign language, history, architecture, and meeting strangers 2. Positive change in self-concept was reported by 63.6 percent 3. Negative change in self-concept was reported by 8.1 percent	

Researcher (year), College and Location	*Sample*	*Instrumentation*
James (1976) U.S. students from various U.S. institutions studying in France	N=52	On-site interviews
Nash (1976) University of Connecticut in France	N=41 (exp grp) N=32 (ctrl grp)	Questionnaire
Price and Hensley (1978) Kent State University Geneva, Switzerland	N=18	Before and after questionnaire
Abrams (1979) Antioch College undergrads	N=330 former study abroad students N=94 (ctrl grp)	

Appendix 2

Findings Related to Personal Change	*Personality Changes Linked to Specific Experience Abroad*
Largest gains reported in self-confidence, self-esteem, appreciation of capability and worth, improved interpersonal skills. Most indicated that they did experience and enjoy a broadening of interest and greater dedication to academic pursuits	
1. Increased autonomy and expansion or differentiation of self 2. No change observed in tolerance, flexibility, or self-confidence 3. Personality changes did not persist after returning home 4. Less favorable attitude toward France	
Modest increases in self-esteem, tolerance of ambiguity, and interest in organizations involving an international orientation	
Study abroad students reported that they felt positive about their experience, they became significantly involved in the host culture, their perceptions of themselves as Americans were challenged, and they were more academically oriented	

Researcher (year), College and Location	*Sample*	*Instrumentation*
Klineburg and Hull (1979)	N=2000 foreign students in 11 countries	1. Questionnaire 2. Interviews
Pelowski (1979) Alumni of Lake Erie College for Women	N=235	1. Interview 2. Questionnaire
Pfnister (1979) Goshen College evaluation of students studying in Third-World countries	Evaluation of past 10 years of study-work abroad	1. Robert Pace General Opinion Survey 2. Interviews
Krawutschke (1980)	N=118	
Marion (1980) University of Colorado	N=90 (follow-up of 1974 study)	Analysis of variance and partial correlations to study the relationship among student characteristics, their activities abroad, and attitude change

Appendix 2

Findings Related to Personal Change	*Personality Changes Linked to Specific Experience Abroad*
Selected findings: foreign students in France were less positive about host country after study abroad	Degree and type of contact
Personal and social growth were cited more often than academic or intellectual outcomes (increased self-confidence)	Quality of the host national family relationship with the student seemed to be the variable that played the most significant role
1. Increased interpersonal skills 2. Increased self-reliance skills 3. Increased self-confidence 4. Possible influence on religious convictions 5. Less concerned about material possessions 6. More tolerant of differences 7. Tightening of student skills in critical thinking	
Ninety-four percent of U.S. institutions face the question of what credit to give for study abroad	
Those who visited more countries became significantly less dogmatic, less conservative, more favorable to host cultures	1. Contact with host culture 2. Location important in shaping view of U.S. 3. Correlation of foreign language ability to view of U.S.

Researcher (year), College and Location	*Sample*	*Instrumentation*
Hopkins (1982)	N=209	1. LSCT (Loevinger Sentence Completion Test) 2. Hawes and Keeley Data Collection and Analysis Instrument
McGhee (1983)		Allen's assessment of Perry position
Koester (1985) students purchasing International Student Identity Card	N=2000 (subsample of larger group)	Questionnaire on impacts of study abroad
Hansel (1986) AFS students	N=1000 (AFS students) N=160 (comparison group)	1. Questionnaire 2. Behaviorally Anchored Rating Scale
Koester (1985)	N=2900 (subsample of sample)	Questionnaire same as above

Appendix 2

Findings Related to Personal Change	*Personality Changes Linked to Specific Experience Abroad*
"Readiness" may be a factor in overseas effectiveness	
Those who start off at lower developmental positions appear to change more than those who begin at higher positions	
Students reported increased political awareness and interest in political events	Type of sojourn Length of sojourn
Students reported an increase in "international awareness"	
Students reported greater interest in international events and in learning, improved sense of self-confidence, greater understanding of U.S.	Type of sojourn Length of sojourn

Researcher (year), College and Location	*Sample*	*Instrumentation*
Koester (1987)	N=15,465	Questionnaire
Carlson and Yachimowicz (1987)	N=366	Questionnaire
Terrell (1982)	N=21	Recorded oral test and writing

Appendix 2

Findings Related to Personal Change	*Personality Changes Linked to Specific Experience Abroad*
Third goal of students was to study language	
First goal of students was to study language	
Average score of students in Mexico entering with one year of Spanish exceeded score of students with two years study on home campus	

BIBLIOGRAPHY

Abrams, I. 1979. "The Impact of Antioch Education through Experience Abroad." *Alternative Higher Education* 3: 176–87.

Abrams, I., and D. B. Arnold. 1967. "The American College and International Education." In *New Dimensions in Higher Education,* no. 27. Washington, DC: U.S. Office of Education, Division of Higher Education.

Abrams-Reis, C. 1980. "Through the Looking Glass and Back Again: What Happens after Return Home?" International Society for Educational, Cultural and Scientific Interchange. *Bulletin of International Interchanges* 15: 9–12.

Adler, P. S. 1975. "The Transition Experience: An Alternative View of Culture Shock." *Journal of Humanistic Psychology* 15: 13–23.

Allport, G. W. 1954. *The Nature of Prejudice.* Cambridge, MA: Addison-Wesley.

Amir, Y. 1969. "Contact Hypothesis in Ethnic Relation." *Psychological Bulletin* 71: 319–43.

Astin, A. W. 1987. "Competition or Cooperation." *Change* 19, no. 5: 12–19.

Augsburger, D. 1986. *Pastoral Counseling across Cultures.* Philadelphia: The Westminster Press.

Bandura, A. 1986. *Social Foundations of Thought and Action: A Social-Cognitive Theory.* Englewood Cliffs, NJ: Prentice-Hall.

Barber, E. 1983. "The Impact of Foreign Educational Experience on Individuals, Comments." International Society for Educational, Cultural and Scientific Interchange. *Bulletin of International Interchanges* 20: 7–10.

Barrows, T. S. 1981. *College Students' Knowledge and Beliefs: A Survey of Global Understanding.* New Rochelle, NY: Change Magazine Press.

Bennett, M. J. 1986a. "Towards Ethnorelativism: A Developmental Model of Intercultural Sensitivity." In *Cross-Cultural Orientation: New Conceptualizations and Applications,* edited by M. P. Paige. Lanham, MD: University Press of America.

Bennett, M. J. 1986b. "A Developmental Approach to Training for Intercultural Sensitivity." *International Journal of Intercultural Relations* 10: 179–96.

Benzler, D. P., and R. A. Schulz. 1979. "Methodological Trends in College Foreign Language Instruction: A Report." *President's Commission on Foreign Language and International Studies.* Washington, DC: U.S. Government Printing Office.

Bereiter, C. 1963. "Some Persisting Dilemmas in the Measurement of Change." In *Problems of Measuring Change,* edited by C. S. Harris. Madison: University of Wisconsin Press.

Billigmeier, R. H., and D. Forman. 1975. "Goettingen in Retrospect." *International Review of Education* 21, no. 2: 217–30.

Bower, T. J. 1973. "Effects of Short Term Study Abroad on Student Attitudes." *Dissertation Abstracts International* 34, 4772-A, University of Colorado, University Microfilm 73–32512.

Bresee, D. E. 1985. "Exchange Program Teenagers Compare Life in Denmark and the U.S.A."*Occasional Papers in Intercultural Learning.* AFS 10: 1–22.

Brislin, R. 1981. *Cross-Cultural Encounters: Face to Face Interaction.* New York: Pergamon.

Brueggemann, W. 1987. *Hope within History.* Atlanta: John Knox Press.

Burnham, W. E., C. A. Trendler, and D. Harris. 1966. Manuscript. "Impact of Foreign Study on American Students." Indiana University.

Carlson, J. S., B. B. Burn, J. Useem, and D. Yachimowicz. 1990. *Study Abroad: The Experience of American Undergraduates in Western Europe and in the United States.* Westport, CT: Greenwood Press.

Carlson, J. S., and C. M. Jensen. 1984. Report. "Evaluation of the University of California's Education Abroad Program: The 1982–83 Participant Questionnaire." University of California, Education Abroad Program, Santa Barbara.

Carlson, J. S., and K. F. Widaman. 1988. "The Effects of Study Abroad during College on Attitudes toward Other Cultures." *International Journal of Intercultural Relations* 8.

Carlson, J. S., and D. Yachimowicz. 1985. Report. "Evaluation of the University of California's Education Abroad Program: The 1983–84 Participant Questionnaire." University of California, Education Abroad Program, Santa Barbara.

Carlson, J. S., and D. Yachimowicz. 1987. Report. "Evaluation of the University of California's Education Abroad Program: The 1986–87 Participant Questionnaire." University of California, Education Abroad Program, Santa Barbara.

Carsello, C., and J. Grieser. 1976. "How College Students Change during Study Abroad." *College Student Journal* 10: 276–78.

Chickering, A. 1969. *Education and Identity*. San Francisco: Jossey-Bass.

Churchill, R. 1958. "The Student Abroad." *Antioch Review* 18: 447–57.

Craig, R. B. 1983. "Changing Student Attitudes through Foreign Study Programs: A Director's Perspective." Paper presented at the annual meeting of the International Society for Educational, Cultural, and Scientific Interchanges, Cincinnati.

Davies, M. W. 1974. "An Investigation of Factors Related to Participant Perception of the Values of Overseas Study." Dissertation, University of Toledo.

Ellison, A, and B. Simon. 1973. "Does College Make a Person Healthy and Wise?" In *Does College Matter?* edited by L. C. Solmon and P. J. Taubman. New York: Academic Press.

Feldman, K. A., ed. 1972. *College and Student*. New York: Pergamon.

Feldman, K. A., and T. M. Newcomb. 1969. *The Impact of College on Students* vol. 1. San Francisco: Jossey-Bass.

Garraty, J. A., and W. Adams. 1959. *From Main Street to Left Bank: Students and Scholars Abroad*. East Lansing: Michigan State University Press.

Goodwin, C. D., and M. Nacht. 1988. *Abroad and Beyond: Patterns in American Overseas Education*. Cambridge, MA: Cambridge University Press.

Gudykunst, W. 1979. "Intercultural Contact and Attitude Change: A View of Literature and Suggestions for Future Research." *International and Intercultural Communication Annual* 4: 1–16.

Gullahorn, J. T., and J. E. Gullahorn. 1963. "An Extension of the U-Cure Hypothesis." *Journal of Social Issues* 14: 33–47.

Hall, F. 1977. *Foreign Students in the United States of America: Coping Behavior within the Educational Environment*. New York: Praeger.

Hansel, B. 1986. The AFS Impact Study: Final Report. *Research Report* 33. New York: AFS International/Intercultural Programs, Research Department.

Hawes, F., and D. J. Kealey. 1981. "An Empirical Study of Canadian Technical Assistance: Adaptation and Effectiveness in Overseas Assignment." *International Journal of Intercultural Relations* 5: 239–58.

Hensley, T. R., and D. K. Sell. 1979. "A Study Abroad Program: Impacts on Student Attitudes." *Teaching Political Science* 6: 387–412.

Hoeh, J. E., and D. Spuck. 1975. "Effects of a Three-Phase Acculturation Process of Language Skill Development and Social and Personal Attitudes of High School French Students." *Foreign Language Annals* 8, no. 3: 220–26.

Hoffman, J. E., and I. Zak. 1969. "Interpersonal Contact and Attitude Change in a Cross-Cultural Situation." *Journal of Social Psychology* 78: 165–71.

Hopkins, R. S. 1982. "Defining and Predicting Overseas Effectiveness for Adolescent Exchange Students." *Dissertation Abstracts International* 42, 12A, 5052 (T-005).

Hosenfeld, C. 1979. "A Language-Teaching View of Second Language Instruction." *Foreign Language Annals* 12: 51.

James, N. W. 1976. "Students Abroad: Expectation versus Reality." *Liberal Education* 42: 559–607.

Kafka, E. P. 1968. "The Effects of Overseas Study on Worldmindedness and Other Selected Variables of Liberal Arts Students." *Dissertation Abstracts* 29, 481A, Michigan State University.

Kauffmann, N. L. 1982. "The Impact of Study Abroad on Personality Change." Dissertation, University of Indiana, 15–20.

Kauffmann, N. L., and G. D. Kuh. 1985. "The Impact of Study Abroad on Personal Development of College Students." *Journal of International Student Personnel,* May.

Keniston, K. 1960. *Youth and Dissent: The Rise of the New Opposition.* New York: Harcourt Brace Jovanovitch.

Kerr, C. 1989. Address given at a conference in Gleneagles, Scotland, on internationalizing the university. Proceedings published 1991 in *American Behavioral Scientist* 35, no. 1, 17–42. Sage Publications.

Kim, H. S. 1988. "The Relationship between Attitudes and Language Proficiency of Korean-Americans Studying in Korea." Master's thesis, Department of Teaching English as a Second Language, University of California, Los Angeles.

Klineburg, O., and F. W. Hull. 1979. *At a Foreign University: International Study of Adaptation and Coping*. New York: Praeger.

Knefelkamp, L. L., and R. A. Sleptiza. 1976. "A Cognitive-Developmental Model of Career Development—An Adaptation of the Perry Scheme." *Counseling Psychologist* 6: 53–58.

Koester, J. 1984. *A Profile of the U.S. Student Abroad*. New York: Council on International Educational Exchange.

Koester, J. 1985. *A Profile of the U.S. Student Abroad*. New York: Council on International Educational Exchange.

Koester, J. 1987. *A Profile of the U.S. Student Abroad—1984 and 1985*. New York: Council on International Educational Exchange.

Krawutschke, E. L. 1980. "U.S. School's Credit Policies for Study Abroad Students: A Survey." *World Higher Education Communique* 2, no. 3: 33–34.

Kuh, G. D., E. J. Whitt, and J. D. Shedd. 1987. "Student Affairs Work, 2001: A Paradigmatic Odyssey." *ACPA Media Publication*.

Lamet, S. A., and M. S. Lamet. 1982. "The Impact of Study Abroad on Selected Groups of Students." Paper presented at the Meeting of the Council on International Educational Exchange, New York.

Lank, H. P. 1983. "Coming Home: An Inquiry into the Reentry Experience of Students Who Studied Abroad." Paper.

Leonard, E. W. 1959. "Selected Liberal Education Outcomes of a Foreign Travel and Study Program." *Dissertation Abstracts*, 1644, Pennsylvania State University, Microfilm 59–5115.

Leonard, E. W. 1964. "Attitude Change in College Program of Study and Travel." *Educational Record* 45: 173–81.

McGhee, M. E. 1983. "An Assessment of the Relation between Study Abroad and Cognitive Development." Master's thesis, Southern Illinois University at Carbondale.

McGuigan, F. J. 1958. "Psychological Changes Related to Intercultural Experiences." *Psychological Reports* 4: 55–60.

McGuigan, F. J. 1959. "Further Study of Psychological Changes Related to Intercultural Experiences." *Psychological Reports* 5:244–48.

Marion, P. B. 1974. "Evaluation of Study Abroad." Paper presented at the annual conference of National Association for Foreign Student Affairs (NAFSA), (ERIC ED 089 634).

Marion, P. B. 1980. "Relations of Student Characteristics and Experiences with Attitude Changes in a Program of Study Abroad." *Journal of College Student Personnel* 21: 58–64.

Martin, J. N. 1986. "Communication in the Intercultural Reentry: Student Sojourners' Perceptions of Change in Reentry Relationships." *International Journal of Intercultural Relations* 10: 1–22.

Martin, J. N. 1987. "The Relationship between Student Sojourners' Perceptions of Intercultural Competence and Previous Sojourn Experience." *International Journal of Intercultural Relations* 11: 337–56.

Mestenhauser, J. A. 1985. "Concepts and Theories of Culture Learning" and "Adding the Disciplines: From Theory to Relevant Practice." In *Culture, Learning, and The Disciplines,* edited by G. Marty and I. Steglitz. Washington, DC: National Association for Foreign Student Affairs.

Morgan, E. E. 1972. "The American College Student in Switzerland: A Study of Cross-Cultural Adaptation and Change." *Dissertation Abstracts International* 33, 592A, University of Pittsburgh.

Nash, D. 1976. "The Personal Consequences of a Year of Study Abroad." *Journal of Higher Education* 47: 191–203.

Newton, F. B., and R. B. Caple. 1985. "Once the World Was Flat: Introduction and Overview." *Journal of Counseling and Development* 64:163–64.

Ong, W. 1969. "World as View and World as Event." *American Anthropologist* 71:4.

Open Doors 1986/87. 1988. New York: Institute for International Education.

Pace, C. R. 1959. "The Junior Year in France: An Evaluation of the University College Program." Syracuse: Syracuse University Press.

Palmer, P. 1987. "Community, Conflict, and Ways of Knowing." *Change* 19: 2.

Parks, S. 1986. *The Critical Years: The Young Adult Search for a Faith to Live By*. San Francisco: Harper and Row.

Pelowski, J. F. 1979. "A Study of the Impact of the Cross-Cultural Education Program, the Winter Term Abroad, on Alumnae of Lake Erie College for Women from 1953 through 1978." Dissertation, Michigan State University, 4, 33.

Perry, W. G. 1970. *Forms of Intellectual and Ethical Development in the College Years*. New York: Holt, Rinehart and Winston.

Pfnister, A. O. 1972. "Impact of Study Abroad on the American College Graduate." University of Denver (ERIC ED 063 882).

Pfnister, A. O. 1979. "Ten-Year Evaluation of Study Service Trimester." Goshen College Office of International Education.

Piaget, J., and B. Inhelder. 1958. *The Growth of Logical Thinking from Childhood to Adolescence*. New York: Basic Books.

Prater, C. H., R. Barrutia, B. D. Larkin, and H. D. Weaver. 1980. *Final Report of the Foreign-Language Review Committee*. University of California, Education Abroad Program, Santa Barbara.

Price, B. L., and T. R. Hensley. 1978. "The Impact on French Students of a Study Abroad Program. The Kent State Experience." Paper presented to the Ohio Modern Language Teachers Association, Columbus, Ohio.

Pyle, K. R. 1981. "International Cross-Cultural Service/Learning: Impact on Student Development." *Journal of College Student Personnel* 22: 509–14.

Salter, C. A., and A. I. Teger. 1975. "Change in Attitudes toward Other Nations as a Function of the Type of International Contact." *Sociometry* 38: 213–22.

Sampson, D. L., and H. P. Smith. 1957. "A Scale to Measure Worldmindedness Attitudes." *The Journal of Social Psychology* 45, 99–106.

Schroeder, C. 1984. "Human Development and the Campus Environment." Paper presented in Peoria, IL.

Sell, D. K. 1981. "Research on Attitude Change among Participants in Foreign Study Experience: Past Findings, a Theoretical Framework, and Prospects for Future Research." Paper presented at the National Association for Foreign Student Affairs, New York, 16.

Sell, D. K. 1983. "Attitude Change in Foreign Study Participants." *International Journal of Intercultural Relations* 7: 131–47.

Sikkema, M., and A. Niyekawa. 1987. *Design for Cross-Cultural Learning*. Yarmouth, ME: Intercultural Press.

Smith, C. T. 1971. "The Relationship of Program Characteristics of the Kalamazoo College Foreign Study Programs to Changes in Participant Attitudes, Values or Interests." *Dissertation Abstracts* 31, 3909A-3910A, University of Michigan, University Microfilm 71–4733.

Smith, H. P. 1957. "The Effects of Intercultural Experience: A Follow-up Investigation." *Journal of Abnormal and Social Psychology* 54: 266–69.

Stauffer, M. L. 1973. "The Impact of Study Abroad Experience on Prospective Teachers." *Dissertation Abstracts International* 34, 2448A, Ohio State University, University Microfilm 73–26, 917.

Terrell, T. 1982. "SAW Program in Mexico." Report. University of California, Education Abroad Program, Santa Barbara.

Treanor, C. C. 1970. "Using Multivariate Statistical Techniques to Assess Change in College Students. *Dissertation Abstracts International* 31, 241A-242A, University of California, Berkeley, University Microfilms 70–13000.

Uehara, A. 1986. "The Nature of American Student Reentry Adjustment and Perceptions of the Sojourn Experience." *International Journal of Intercultural Relations* 10, no. 4: 415–38.

Weaver, H. D., ed. 1989. *Research on U.S. Students Abroad*. New York: Council on International Educational Exchange.

Weissman, D., and A. Furnham. 1987. "The Expectations and Experiences of a Sojourning Temporary Resident Abroad: A Preliminary Study." *Human Relations* 40, no. 5:313–26.

Westerhoff, J. H., III. 1976. *Will Our Children Have Faith*? New York: The Seabury Press.

Winter, O., O. McClelland, and A. Stewart. 1981. *A New Case for the Liberal Arts*. San Francisco: Jossey-Bass.